DAVID WILLIAMSON was
and brought up in Bairnsdale
a graduate in Mechanical Er
versity and was a lecturer in thermodynamics and
chology at Swinburne Institute of Technology until 1973.
His first full-length play, *The Coming of Stork,* had its pre-
mière at the La Mama Theatre, Carlton, in 1970 and later
became the film *Stork,* directed by Tim Burstall.

But it was his next two plays which together established
him as Australia's most sought-after dramatic writer. *The
Removalists* and *Don's Party,* both written in 1971, were
quickly taken up and performed around Australia, then in
London and later made into films with screenplays by the
author. *The Removalists* won the British George Devine
Award in 1971 for the Nimrod Street production in Sydney;
and in 1972 the Australian Writers Guild Awgie Awards for
the best stage play and the best script in any medium. In
1973 David Williamson was nominated the most promising
playwright by the London *Evening Standard* following the
British production of *The Removalists.*

The next play was *Jugglers Three* (1972) commissioned by
the Melbourne Theatre Company; followed by *What If You
Died Tomorrow* (1973) for the Old Tote Theatre Company;
The Department (1975) and *A Handful of Friends* (1976) for
the South Australian Theatre Company. *The Club* (1977)
broke all previous box office records and in 1978 had sea-
sons at the Kennedy Centre, Washington, on Broadway and
in Berlin. In 1980 the Nimrod Theatre production went to
London. The film, directed by Bruce Beresford, was released
in 1980. *Travelling North* was performed round Australia in
1979 and in London in 1980. It was followed by *Celluloid
Heroes* (1980), *The Perfectionist* (1982), *Sons of Cain* (1985)
and *Emerald City* (1987).

David Williamson has won the Australian Film Institute
film script award for *Petersen* (1974), *Don's Party* (1976) and
Gallipoli (1981). Recent scripts include *Phar Lap* (1985),
Travelling North (1987), *Emerald City* (1988), the TV mini-
series *The Last Bastion* (1985), *A Dangerous Life* (1988), *The
Four Minute Mile* (1988) and the telemovie *The Perfectionist*
(1985). He lives in Sydney with his journalist wife Kristin and
four children.

Jon Ewing as Warren Belconnen and Max Cullen as Kevin Cassidy in the Royal Queensland Theatre Company production. Photo: Ian Poole.

CURRENCY PLAYS
General Editor: Katharine Brisbane

First published in 1985
by Currency Press Pty Ltd,
PO Box 452, Paddington,
N.S.W. 2021, Australia.
Revised 1988.

National Library of Australia Cataloguing-in-Publication data:

Williamson, David, 1942-
    Sons of Cain.

    Rev. ed.
    ISBN 0 86819 179 5.

    I. Title.

A822'.3

Typeset and printed by Bridge Printery Pty Ltd, Rosebery 2018.
Cover design by Kevin Chan

Currency's creative writing program is assisted by the
Australia Council, the Federal Government's arts funding
and advisory body.

Sons of Cain

David Williamson

CURRENCY PRESS · SYDNEY

The cry of the Little Peoples goes up to God in vain
For the world is given over to the cruel Sons of Cain.

Richard Le Gallienne (1866-1947)
The Cry of the Little Peoples

By the same author

SONS OF CAIN

John Noble, Director, and Max Cullen outside Wyndham's Theatre in London during the 1986 season.

Above: Sandy Gore as Nicole, Genevieve Picot as Bronwen, Max Cullen as Kevin and Liddy Clark as Crystal. MTC production. Photo: David Parker. Below: Debbie Whatley as Bronwen, Judith Stevenson as Nicole, Marilyn Hanigan as Crystal, Norman Coburn as Rex Harding and Terry Kenwrick as Kevin. Darwin Theatre Group production. Photo: Jude Swift.

Above: Noel Ferrier as Warren Belconnen. Below: Sandy Gore as Nicole and Liddy Clark as Crystal. Melbourne Theatre Company production. Photos: David Parker.

Sons of Cain was first performed by the Melbourne Theatre Company at the Playhouse of the Victorian Arts Centre, Melbourne, on 26 March 1985 with the following cast:

GARY QUEST	Ray Barrett
KEVIN CASSIDY	Max Cullen
REX HARDING	John Gregg
WARREN BELCONNEN	Noel Ferrier
CRYSTAL	Liddy Clark
NICOLE	Sandy Gore
BRONWEN	Genevieve Picot
LAURIE BYRNE	John Clayton

Directed by David Williamson
Designed by Shaun Gurton
Lighting designed by Jamie Lewis
Dramaturg, Wayne Harrison

CHARACTERS

GARY QUEST, Labor Premier of an Australian State
RICHARD, an off-screen TV interviewer
KEVIN CASSIDY, editor of the *Weekly Review*
REX HARDING, managing editor of the *Weekly Review*
WARREN BELCONNEN, a media baron
CRYSTAL
NICOLE } investigative journalists
BRONWEN
LAURIE BYRNE, a retired police officer

All characters in this play are fictitious and any resemblance to any person living or dead is purely coincidental.

PROLOGUE

A face, back projected and magnified to giant proportions, is seen on a large screen that is an integral part of the design. The face is that of the Premier, GARY QUEST. *When the audience lights dim the face suddenly comes alive. An off-screen interviewer asks questions. The interviewer is known as* RICHARD.

RICHARD: *[off]* Do you intend to hold an enquiry, Mr Quest?

QUEST: No, I don't, Richard. There have been more than enough enquiries in this State without me wasting tax-payers' money on another one.

RICHARD: There's been a lot of press speculation —

QUEST: If I listened to all the hyenas of the press there'd be an enquiry called every day of the week. Laurie Byrne resigned from the police force of his own volition for reasons of a private nature related to his health.

RICHARD: The press suggest that Byrne might have been squeezed out of the Force because he was too honest.

QUEST: The press are experts at hinting at impropriety and never offering a shred of proof.

RICHARD: So there will be no enquiry?

QUEST: There certainly won't. Not while I'm Premier of this State.

SCENE ONE

The image of QUEST *fades from the large screen and is replaced by an image of a spectacular view. We are in* REX's *office and the view is from his window.* REX *paces around his office.* KEVIN *sits in a chair watching him.* KEVIN *is a shambling bear of a man who seems to have been randomly assembled from a scrap heap of skeletal parts. His accent is flat and nasal, but he articulates with precision and an understated deadpan irony. The clothes he wears do nothing to enhance his appearance. In contrast,* REX *is stylishly dressed in a modern suit which sits well on*

his neat frame. He is urbane and seemingly confident but we
sense it's a carefully constructed act. There is a constant thread
of anxiety and insecurity underlying his public persona.

KEVIN: Commanding view, Rex.

REX: One of the perks of moving up into upper management.
    [*Pause*]
    I suppose you guessed I didn't ask you here to admire the
    view.

KEVIN: It crossed my mind.

REX: [*embarrassed*] I've been meaning to get in touch for ages.
    The trouble with the lifestyle I'm enmeshed in at the mo-
    ment is that the only time you get to eat with people is to
    talk deals.

KEVIN: Right.

REX: I meant to ring when I heard about you and Margaret
    splitting up. Must have been hard for you both.

KEVIN: It wasn't fun.

REX: You both OK now, though?

KEVIN: She's fine.

REX: She's not depressed any more?

KEVIN: No.

REX: Great.

KEVIN: She's as happy as Larry.

REX: I always had a feeling you were never quite right for
    each other.

KEVIN: Did you?

REX: Yes.

KEVIN: Is that why you propositioned her?

REX: I didn't proposition her.

KEVIN: You groped her leg through a whole dinner party.
    She told me.

REX: I did that a lot in those days. I was a shit.

KEVIN: You've changed?

REX: Yes, I have.
    [KEVIN *looks unconvinced.*]

KEVIN: Why did you get the feeling we were never quite right
    for each other?

REX: I thought she married too young.

KEVIN: She's two years younger than me.

REX: You were very mature. An abrasive no-nonsense journalist. You dazzled her.

KEVIN: But if she'd looked past the veneer she'd have realised that I wasn't worth the effort.

REX: You're still a difficult man to have a conversation with, Kevin.

KEVIN: Jesus, you ask me if she's still depressed. What about me? I'm depressed as hell.

REX: I'm sorry.

KEVIN: I wouldn't have got half so paranoid and possessive if all my old friends hadn't taken her to bed, or tried to take her to bed, or rubbed their bloody fat hands all over her thighs under tables.

[*Pause.*]

REX: Who took her to bed?

KEVIN: I'd rather not talk about it.

REX: I was just curious.

[*Pause.*]

I bet it was Peter Sutton.

KEVIN: Of course it was Peter Sutton.

REX: Peter had a lot of polish.

KEVIN: Why wouldn't the prick have polish? If four generations of Melbourne Grammar can't knock the convict out of you, then a lot of people have been wasting their money.

REX: Last time I heard of Peter he was in trouble over selling shonky tax schemes.

KEVIN: I know. I wrote the piece that nailed him.

REX: Look, the reason I asked you over —

KEVIN: She told me we had nothing to talk about together any more, so we went out to dinner and she was right. All I'm interested in is my work and she doesn't want to know about it. I can't talk to Alan, either. We run out of things to say.

REX: How old is he now?

KEVIN: Nine.

[*He fishes in his wallet.*]

I've got a photo. I took him kicking a football last week-

end, which for someone in my physical condition is
bloody near heroic.

[KEVIN *hands* REX *the snapshot.*]

He looked at me and said, 'Geez, Dad, you look shithouse
in shorts.' The kid wasn't wrong. I've got this vein like the
great arctic pipeline going down my leg.

REX: [*looking at the photo*] Great kid.

KEVIN: 'So I'm not an attractive human being', I said to him,
'The genetic dice gave me a lousy throw.'

REX: Kevin, the reason I asked —

KEVIN: [*cutting in*] I probably didn't try hard enough to stop
her but I never thought I'd miss her so much.

REX: I'm sorry about groping her thigh. It makes me cringe
to think about it.

KEVIN: Don't be so pious. You're forty-four, you can't get it
up as often and suddenly you're Mr Sensitive.

REX: Still the total cynic.

KEVIN: Well, Jesus Christ, you finally learnt to keep your
paws off every passing female and you think it qualifies
you for sainthood.

REX: I *have* changed. I was insensitive and sexist and I
squirm whenever I'm reminded of it. I know where I was
then and where I am now and I've come a long way. A
very long way.

KEVIN: You still seem to be crawling up the Establishment
arsehole like a dung beetle.

REX: All right, Kevin. Thanks for coming. See you again,
sometime. You know your way out.

KEVIN: It's true! In the old days you never left off bashing my
ears about the poor and the under-privileged. When you
got power, why didn't you do something about it?

REX: I started the *Review*.

KEVIN: The *Review?*

REX: Can you name any other faintly radical journal in the
country?

KEVIN: No. It's absolutely *the* most faintly radical journal we
have.

REX: Goodbye, Kevin. Thank you for coming.

KEVIN: The *Review* is bland and gutless.

REX: Do something about it, then.

KEVIN: The *Review?*

REX: Edit it. That's why I got you here. To ask you to edit it.

KEVIN: Edit it?

REX: It *is* too bland. Whatever intentions I had when I started it, it's drifted — it's not getting anybody excited any more. Corruption has reached epidemic proportions in this country and I want an editor who's gutsy enough to hit at the bastards who are turning this country into a sewer. Does that sound like the offer of a grovelling dung beetle?

KEVIN: What's happened to Ian?

REX: I've sacked him. Kevin, you know as well as I do how bad things are. Politicians, lawyers, the judiciary, the police force, business — they're all in it up to their necks. The problem's so massive it's hard to know where to start. Listen to me, when Laurie Byrne was tossed out of the police force for being too honest and Gary Quest — well, you must have seen him on the news last night —

[KEVIN *nods.*]

Well, that finished me. I felt as angry and sick in the stomach as you must've. I went and levelled the same charges at myself as you've just levelled, and decided that I had to do something about it. I love this country, Kevin, or more correctly I love what this country could be. I'm sick to death of the muck, the cynicism and the lies, and when I looked in the mirror last night I said to myself, what the fuck do you want to end up life having achieved? You're on nodding terms with the wealthy and the powerful. Fantastic. You've flashed your gold credit card in the best hotel foyers in the world. Big deal. You've seen everything from the Ming tombs to the temples of Samarkand. So what? So bloody what? When back here in your own culture you wince every time a politician appears on television because you know he's either just lied or is about to. Kevin, *we* are in a position to grab the helm and change course, and just remember *who* and *what* is backing us. Warren Belconnen controls a third of the media power in this country and he is *unconditionally* committed. I fought him to get the *Review* started but he's backed me to the hilt ever since and he'll back me on this one. I want you to edit the toughest, gutsiest, most incisive paper that's ever been published in this country and I won't be satisfied until you're getting three death threats a week and there's fifty million dollars' worth of lawsuits pending. What do you say?

KEVIN: No.

REX: Mate, come on. Do you want to know some facts about the organisation of the drug trade in this country?

KEVIN: I know all you can tell me and more.

REX: And you don't care?

KEVIN: Do you know what the life expectancy of a journalist is?

REX: No.

KEVIN: Yeah, well, you haven't got long to go and I'm living on borrowed time. Do you know how long it would take me to make a *dent* in corruption in this country? Three bloody lifetimes. Why didn't you offer this job to me ten years ago, you moral johnny-come-fucking-lately, instead of waiting until my vital organs are chatting amongst themselves about who's going to pack it in first. *You* listen to *me* this time. I could have *done* something when I had the energy, the stamina and the brain cells to bloody well do the job properly and there wouldn't have been half the shit going on in this country if I had.

REX: Mate, you're not over the hill yet.

KEVIN: I couldn't make it up the bloody hill.

REX: Mate . . .

KEVIN: *Mate,* I find it *disgusting* that you've taken this long to look in your mirror and if you think I'm about to spend the last few years of my life making you feel that your life has been worthwhile, forget it.

REX: You just want me to throw this opportunity away?

KEVIN: Get someone else to edit it.

REX: Who?

[*A long pause.*]

KEVIN: I'd want a contract that was so iron tight you, Warren or anybody on earth couldn't get rid of me for at least a year. And I want the present staff to be supplemented by three new appointments of my choice. Your present staff can keep doing adventure, travel and health foods. These three do what I want 'em to do.

[*Pause.*]

And I want to be paid *heaps.* Warren's got to realise that turning this country into a moral paradise isn't cheap. OK?

REX: Mate, I'm feeling better now than I have for twenty years.

KEVIN: That'd be right. You've just condemned me to three death threats a week and a premature grave and spent someone else's money doing it.

SCENE TWO

WARREN BELCONNEN'*s office. The view from the window is even better than* REX'*s office.* WARREN *is pacing around.* REX *is standing still.* WARREN *is a large, powerful man with a manner of total authority. He is an uncrowned prince of the land. Politicians may think they rule but* WARREN *knows that he does.*

WARREN: He's a drunk. I sacked him once, didn't I?

REX: No.

WARREN: If I didn't I should've.

REX: He's cut back on his drinking.

WARREN: How often have I heard that one? 'He's cut back on his drinking'. So why does he keep banging into walls? Why is this profession littered with drunks, Rex?

REX: I —

WARREN: You know what I think it is? I think it's because it attracts misfits and bums. Seething with free-floating hostility. The only way they can stand themselves is to get drunk. I'd really enjoy the newspaper business if it wasn't for journalists. Isn't there anyone else?

REX: Milton Carstairs?

WARREN: Wiltin' Milton? You've got to be joking. The subs call him 'Cowshit' — comes out steaming and falls in a heap.

REX: Yes, I agree. The one thing about Kevin is that he doesn't lack guts.

WARREN: This bloody *Review* of yours has been the bane of my life, Rex. Hasn't made a cent in ten years.

REX: Given us a lot of prestige.

WARREN: Prestige, my arse.

REX: No one can claim we just publish tits and bums.

WARREN: Every bloody dinner party I go to some smart arse asks me, 'How's the *Review?* Circulation up yet?'

REX: We'll get it up when we start in on corruption.

WARREN: You'd better. If it weren't for you, Rex, I'd have closed the darn thing years ago. What about that Greg Gibson fellow?

REX: Greg's a good man.

WARREN: But what?

REX: [*shrugging*] Oh, we all say things when we've had a drink too many.

WARREN: What did the bastard say?

REX: It doesn't do anyone any good to pass that sort of thing on.

WARREN: What did he say?

REX: He says you bought yourself power by appealing to the lowest common denominator.

WARREN: That almost makes me want to appoint him. So I can give him buggery for twelve months. What does Kevin say about me?

REX: Kevin's attitude is very positive. He said to me that if it weren't for you backing the *Review,* this country would have no investigative press whatsoever.

WARREN: All I've heard about him is that he's a bloody trouble maker. But if you want him, you have him. You two make all the decisions about what you're going to publish. Don't come running to me. All I want to see are results.

REX: You'll get 'em, Warren. You'll get 'em.

SCENE THREE

KEVIN's *office in the main office area. It is small and does not have a view. A video display terminal sits on the desk.* KEVIN *circles it suspiciously, prods it, and finally pushes it along the desk and gives pride of place to a battered old manual typewriter he has removed from its case.* CRYSTAL *knocks on the door and enters. She is a bright, pleasant, ebullient woman in her thirties.*

CRYSTAL: Sorry I'm late.
   [*Pause.*]
  I'm Crystal Johnson.
KEVIN: Ah. Yes. Sit down.
   [*Pause.*]
  I've read your stuff.
CRYSTAL: And?
KEVIN: You can't write.
CRYSTAL: [*her smile hardening*] You mean I can't write the sort of threadbare journalism you're used to.
KEVIN: No. I meant you can't write. You use five times as many words as you need and even then I haven't got a clue what you're trying to say.
CRYSTAL: Perhaps that's your problem.
KEVIN: I'm no fool and if I can't understand what you're saying lady, you've got problems.
CRYSTAL: What I've got is a first-class honours degree in Philosophy and English. You've got the problem.
KEVIN: I took years to recover from academic brilliance too. Now if you want to learn to write —
CRYSTAL: I *can* write.
KEVIN: What's the circulation of your journal lady?
CRYSTAL: Circulation isn't one of our main preoccupations.
KEVIN: You don't care if nobody reads it?
CRYSTAL: It's a specialist journal aimed at opinion leaders.
KEVIN: Thank you for coming to see me. I wish you and your journal all the best.
CRYSTAL: They all told me I was wasting my time.

KEVIN: Lady —

CRYSTAL: [*interrupting him as she leaves*] I am *not* a *lady*.

KEVIN: Why did you answer the ad?

CRYSTAL: Because I was stupid enough to believe that you *were* looking for intelligence and incisiveness. I should have realised that anything published by Warren Belconnen would be more of the same.

KEVIN: Lady —

CRYSTAL: Don't call me *lady*.

KEVIN: I'll call you what I bloody well want to call you, and you can do the same. Your journal's a wank written by academics trying to impress each other. If you want to have any *real* impact out there you're going to have to learn to *write*.

CRYSTAL: I'm not interested in learning to write popularised, watered-down pap.

KEVIN: Neither am I. You can be as tough as you bloody well like but if you want to be *effective* you've got to stop hiding behind abstract rhetoric and use concrete examples. Theory is the refuge of intellectual charlatans.

CRYSTAL: If you've finished your anti-intellectual tirade I'll go.

KEVIN: You've got a load of aggression and a good deal of intelligence and you could be doing something far more useful than telling five hundred of the converted that men are beasts and women are downtrodden. We all know that by now, lady.

CRYSTAL: My name is Crystal.

KEVIN: Who the hell was vicious enough to call you that?

CRYSTAL: *I* called me that. My parents called me Christine.

KEVIN: What's wrong with that? Mine called me Kevin.

CRYSTAL: There's nothing wrong with Kevin.

KEVIN: Nothing at all. It's like having a sign around your neck saying, 'I am an Irish mick with no social graces and a festering hate of humanity.' What's wrong with Christine?

CRYSTAL: They get pregnant at seventeen and marry Kevins. I don't happen to think that what I'm writing now is irrelevant, especially when what you're offering is up-market muckraking.

KEVIN: Muckraking?

CRYSTAL: When you strip away the glamour isn't that what investigative journalism is?

KEVIN: Point one. There is no glamour in investigative journalism. Point two. Without journalism that's prepared to look beyond press releases corruption runs riot. Scrutiny is the only thing that makes the big boys careful and we don't have much scrutiny in this country because the press is owned by three men who aren't very motivated to scrutinise. I've been given a chance to exchange a little torch with three volt batteries for a bloody great searchlight. And I'm going to use it to try and make this country a little more honest. If you reckon that's muckraking then you can just piss off.

CRYSTAL: The only hope for a better world is to sweep away male power hierarchies and replace them with female organisational forms of trust and cooperation.

KEVIN: Like Maggie Thatcher thumping the Argentinians?

CRYSTAL: She's a woman trapped in a male power structure.

KEVIN: Crystal, women *won't* be running the world for quite a while because your average insensitive male is much more interested in power and how to grab it than your average female. And because he wants it so much, he's better at getting it. He knows when to fight and when to keep quiet and when to suck up to his bosses. He's a very dangerous animal, and in countries where there *isn't* a free press, the top males end up with so *much* power they make life unbearable for everyone else. If you want to make sure that doesn't happen here, then I'm offering you the chance.

CRYSTAL: If I can't write, and you despise my beliefs, why are you offering me the job?

KEVIN: I'm not.

CRYSTAL: You just said, 'If you don't want it to happen here I'm offering you the chance.'

KEVIN: I was speaking metaphorically.

CRYSTAL: So you're not offering me the job?

KEVIN: You said you didn't want it.

CRYSTAL: If I do, are you offering it to me?

KEVIN: Do you want it?

CRYSTAL: Yes.
KEVIN: All right, then.
CRYSTAL: I can't start right away.
KEVIN: No hurry. No hurry at all.

SCENE FOUR

KEVIN's *office some time later.* KEVIN *is interviewing* NICOLE, *a very attractive woman in her late thirties. She is dressed in a manner that would do credit to the pages of* Vogue *magazine. She is cool, controlled and keeps her emotions in check. She doesn't particularly like men, perhaps because she's been given little cause to, and finds it wearisome to have to pander to their egos, although when she has to, she can do it with skill. She far prefers to undercut them subtly — so subtly that they can never accuse her of outright aggression.*

KEVIN: I've read a lot of your work over the years, Nicole. You write well.
NICOLE: It's reassuring to hear someone of your standing say so, Kevin. I sometimes lose confidence.
KEVIN: Your work's fine. You get straight to the core and don't waste words.
NICOLE: I'm pleased you think so. I've been an admirer of your work for a long time.
KEVIN: Why did you apply for this job?
NICOLE: I feel as if I've painted myself into a corner at the *Mail*. I'd like to do work that had real impact. Many applicants?
KEVIN: Most of the ones you'd expect. I didn't expect you.
NICOLE: Does that put me out of the running?
KEVIN: You'd be taking a step backwards, wouldn't you?
NICOLE: Why do you say that?
KEVIN: This job can be pretty boring. You won't be writing editorials or shaping the nation's future.
NICOLE: Who reads editorials? I'd rather be back on hard fea-

tures, Kevin. Are you worried I've lost my edge?

KEVIN: No. I don't want anyone who's been doing hard stuff too long. They're usually burnt out.

NICOLE: If I'm a bit rusty, I'm sure you'll be able to point me in the right direction.

KEVIN: Are you concerned about what's going on around you?

NICOLE: Corruption? Certainly.

KEVIN: How concerned?

NICOLE: Very. I'm disgusted by how blatant it is.
    [*Pause.*]

KEVIN: How do you *really* feel?

NICOLE: About corruption? I don't lose a lot of sleep over it but I'm totally professional, and if you think corruption's important I'll make myself lose some sleep over it.

SCENE FIVE

KEVIN'*s office some time later. He is interviewing* BRONWEN, *a slight, nervous woman in her twenties. She has an intensity about her that springs from a deep commitment to idealistic causes. She regards her physical appearance as unimportant, but still manages to look fresh and appealing, despite an odd, almost random, assortment of clothes.*

KEVIN: You haven't exactly had a stunning career to date, Bronwen.

BRONWEN: No.

KEVIN: It's a bit hard to get the feel of your prose style from the daily court listings.
    [*Pause.*]
How long have you been working for Brian?

BRONWEN: Four years.

KEVIN: Has he tried you on features or interviews?

BRONWEN: He gave me a few interviews.

KEVIN: Not published?

BRONWEN: No.

KEVIN: Why?

BRONWEN: He said they were insipid.

KEVIN: Were they?

BRONWEN: Possibly. I think I was supposed to do a hatchet job on two of them.

KEVIN: But you didn't?

BRONWEN: No. I admired them both.

KEVIN: Bronwen, as much as I'd like to help, it's a bit hard to justify taking you on . . .

BRONWEN: I'm sure I can do it.

KEVIN: I'm sure you can too but . . .

BRONWEN: I hate what's going on in this State at the moment and I want to do something about it.

KEVIN: What sort of things make you angry?

BRONWEN: The drug trade and people like Laurie Byrne getting tossed out of the police force.

KEVIN: Do you know why he was tossed out?

BRONWEN: He wanted to clean up the drug squad. Half of them were dealing in heroin.

KEVIN: *Five* of them were.

BRONWEN: Rather than rock the boat they got rid of him.

KEVIN: It's a bit more sordid than that. Someone more senior than Laurie was getting a rake off. The rotten thing about this job, Bronwen, is that you know so much and can print so little. Can you cope with that sort of frustration?

BRONWEN: Yes.

KEVIN: Okay, Bronwen. Against my better judgement I'll give you a go.

BRONWEN: Thanks. I won't let you down.

SCENE SIX

REX's *office.* KEVIN *sits on his desk reading a newspaper.* REX *enters.*

REX: Ah. Thanks for coming. Take a seat.

KEVIN: [*thrusting the paper towards him*] Recognise anyone?
REX: No.
   [*He shakes his head.*]
KEVIN: If you can't pick the face, try the thigh.
REX: [*as it dawns on him*] That's your wife, Margaret.
KEVIN: Never forgets a kneecap.
REX: Hey, doesn't she look great? Is that the new boyfriend?
KEVIN: No. That one.
REX: Fit looking bugger, isn't he?
KEVIN: I get a knock on my door the other night and there's Margaret with young Alan. 'You'll have to have him for a few weeks' she says, 'Nick and I couldn't live with ourselves if we didn't do something to try and save the rain forests.'
REX: Why are they all wearing lap-laps?
KEVIN: [*sourly*] Children of nature and all that sort of shit. I said that if she and Nick got their kicks lying in front of bulldozers, that's fine, but I was just starting a new job and much as I love my son I just couldn't have him.
REX: What did she say?
KEVIN: She just said I had to and left. And to finish me off young Alan sees the paper this morning and says, 'Hey, Mum's famous.' You wanted to see me about something?
REX: Your appointments.
KEVIN: What's wrong with them?
REX: Well, this Crystal — is that right?
KEVIN: Yes. Crystal as in 'clear as'.
REX: She's apparently written nothing except feminist theory in some obscure journal.
KEVIN: That's right.
REX: What are her qualifications for a job like this?
KEVIN: She hates men.
REX: Be serious, will you, *mate*. My head's on the line over this exercise.
KEVIN: I need motivated staff. She hates men. Men are responsible for corruption.
REX: What motivation fires Nicole?
KEVIN: She hates everybody.
REX: You're playing with fire there, mate.

KEVIN: She's smart and she can write.

REX: She can also cause a lot of trouble. A *lot* of trouble. Sweet as pie to your face but lethal behind your back.

KEVIN: She's never done anything to me.

REX: Do you know what she calls you?

KEVIN: I can imagine.

REX: The last of the macho illiterates.

KEVIN: She'll keep.

REX: It's bloody embarrassing for me to have her here.

KEVIN: Why?

REX: I sacked her when she was working for me six or seven years ago.

KEVIN: Turned you down, did she?

REX: No. She turned a close knit group of working colleagues into a piranha pit in less than a year. On to anything yet?

KEVIN: After two days?

REX: My head's on the line. We need to get results soon.

KEVIN: We couldn't miss. Right at the moment the chances are some constable's out there paying cash for a Lamborghini.

REX: We can't print anything without facts and figures.

KEVIN: There is evidence out there but we can't use it.

REX: What evidence?

KEVIN: The cops run phone taps on every crooked lawyer in town.

REX: Legal taps.

KEVIN: No.

REX: They're tapping phones illegally?

KEVIN: They use the information to bust drug rings. I'd give an arm and a leg to get my hands on some of those transcripts.

SCENE SEVEN

The main office area of the Review. *Video display units are everywhere.* KEVIN *talks to* NICOLE, CRYSTAL *and* BRONWEN.

KEVIN: Forget the Hollywood bullshit. Investigative journalism is about as exciting as watching your fingernails grow. After you've done thousands of company searches and land title searches you'll know what I mean.
[*Pause.*]
You'll have to force yourselves to ring people who've told you ten times already they never want to hear your voice again. And pretend you know a hell of a lot more than you do in the hope they'll let something slip.
[*Pause.*]
If you *do* manage to get something published in the face of our draconian libel laws the chances are it'll never lead to a conviction because proving corruption legally is bloody near impossible.

CRYSTAL: Why?

KEVIN: No proof. Nothing's ever written down. In an assault or robbery there are victims who'll testify; but the guy who *gives* the bribe and the guy who *accepts* the bribe are more than happy with their deal. The only victim of corruption is society itself. What the population out there don't realise, or refuse to realise, is that in the end it's everybody who pays.

CRYSTAL: Now tell us the good news.

KEVIN: There ain't none. The thing that finally depresses the hell out of you in this game is that you get to know the names of all the drug wholesalers, the vice kings, the lot. And you know the chances are they'll probably never cop as much as a parking ticket.

BRONWEN: I'd like to talk to that cop who was thrown out of the force.

NICOLE: Laurie Byrne.

KEVIN: You'll be wasting your time but you're welcome to try.

SCENE EIGHT

The backyard of a house. BRONWEN *and* NICOLE *are talking to* LAURIE BYRNE.

BRONWEN: Mr Byrne, some people have said that your dis-
    missal proves the old adage that in every barrel there are
    one or two good apples.
LAURIE: There's a lot more honest cops than dishonest ones.
    That's something your boss'll never believe, but it's true.
BRONWEN: How do you feel about the Force now?
LAURIE: The Force has given me the best years of my life. I
    was a street kid without a dad and the Force gave me dig-
    nity and mates and a job that helped a lot more people
    than it ever hurt.
NICOLE: The same Force has you ignominiously thrown out of
    your job, Mr Byrne.
LAURIE: The Force didn't throw me out. I was shafted by a
    handful of crooked cops at the top.
BRONWEN: We want to help you get rid of them.
LAURIE: Print their names and the law suits'll wipe you out.
BRONWEN: We don't need names. If you just give us your
    story we'll print what's going on.
LAURIE: Gary Quest will just go on television and say it's
    smear and innuendo.
NICOLE: And that he has complete faith in his police force.
BRONWEN: It's been rumoured that a very high ranking offi-
    cer in the Force was getting a pay-off from your drug
    squad. Did you come across any evidence of that?
LAURIE: No.
BRONWEN: Do you know where we might find evidence?
LAURIE: No.
BRONWEN: But you've said to us that you were shafted by
    crooked cops at the top.
LAURIE: That was off the record.
BRONWEN: Will you say something on the record?
LAURIE: No.

BRONWEN: You retired for health reasons?

LAURIE: Yes.

BRONWEN: How is it that some high ranking police officers have huge houses and big boats?

LAURIE: They win at the races.

BRONWEN: They never lose?

LAURIE: No. It's amazing how your luck changes when you get to the top.

BRONWEN: Everyone in the State seems to know the *real* reason you left the Force, Mr Byrne, I just find it incredible that nothing can be done.

NICOLE: There are a lot of powerful people who *want* nothing to be done.

LAURIE: You start unearthing connections and you never know where they might lead.

BRONWEN: Why doesn't the *public* demand something's done?

NICOLE: Montaigne said, 'There is no state so bad that it is not preferable to change and disturbance.'

BRONWEN: Well, I'm going to bloody well be a disturber.

NICOLE: Thanks, Mr Byrne.

SCENE NINE

The main office area. CRYSTAL *sits at her video display terminal. She utters a cry of alarm followed by a cry of rage.* NICOLE *enters.*

NICOLE: Something wrong?

CRYSTAL: I pushed the wrong button and wiped the whole story.

[NICOLE *goes to her aid and starts pressing buttons.*]

Imagine if Shakespeare had to work these monstrosities. Gets to the last line of *Hamlet* and pushes the wrong button.

NICOLE: There.

CRYSTAL: [*delighted*] It's back. You're a genius, how'd you do it?

NICOLE: I pressed what's known colloquially as the 'drongo button'. Gives you three minutes' grace before wipe out.

CRYSTAL: Do you like working on these things?

NICOLE: They save time.

CRYSTAL: How'd you go with the policeman?

NICOLE: Nothing. But then I expected it.

CRYSTAL: Where do you go now?

NICOLE: God knows.

CRYSTAL: Kevin's got a good track record for ferreting out embarrassing facts, hasn't he?

NICOLE: Not since the manila envelope story. Kevin had Mr Big and the Police Commissioner dining together in a back room in Chinatown and a big fat manila envelope was supposed to have changed hands.

CRYSTAL: It didn't?

NICOLE: If it did, it defied all known laws of physics. The Commissioner was there two days before Mr Big.

CRYSTAL: Bad mistake.

NICOLE: Yeah. Kevin claimed he was set up. A lot of other journos think his habit of print first, check after, might have finally caught up with him.
[*Pause.*]
I liked the work in your journal.

CRYSTAL: You read it?
[NICOLE *nods.*]
Bit esoteric.

NICOLE: I thought it was right on the cutting edge of feminist theory.

CRYSTAL: A lot of my 'sisters' thought it was pretty middle of the road.

NICOLE: You'll find some entrenched male chauvinism around here.

CRYSTAL: [*nodding*] According to Kevin, male power structures are here to stay and that's that.

NICOLE: Kevin is the last of the macho illiterates.
[KEVIN *and* BRONWEN *enter his office.*]

KEVIN: You don't like the idea?

[BRONWEN *sits, tight-lipped, and stares at the wall.*]

I take it that means no.

BRONWEN: I came here to tackle corruption not to do articles on food preservatives.

KEVIN: There's a lot of harm being done to people by food preservatives.

BRONWEN: There's a lot of harm being done to people by sunshine. I just don't happen to want to write about it.

[*Pause.*]

KEVIN: That's not a bad idea.

BRONWEN: What?

KEVIN: Sunshine. A good skin cancer article can double your sales in Queensland.

BRONWEN: How to live with your melanoma?

[*She stares at the wall again.*]

KEVIN: Bronwen, writing on corruption's a bit like fishing. You've got to sit and wait. Someone with a score to settle gives you a starting point.

[BRONWEN *continues to stare at the wall.*]

Bronwen, stop sitting there trying to intimidate me with body langauge.

[*The phone rings.* KEVIN *picks it up, looking irritated.*]

Speaking. Thanks for ringing back. I'm young Alan's dad. He said you yelled at him yesterday because he forgot a library book.

[*Pause.*]

Well, he said 'yelled'. I just wanted to say it wasn't his fault.

[*Pause.*]

Well, he said 'yelled'— he was very upset.

[*Pause.*]

Whether you do or not, it wasn't his fault. I pushed the poor kid off to school before he was ready because I was trying to listen to the news and his mother is up stopping bulldozers. And while I've got you there, lady . . . *Look*, I'll call you what I bloody-well like. He's a slow reader but he's not dumb.

[*Pause.*]

Well, if you didn't use the word you certainly conveyed
the feeling. Any system that makes a great little kid like
that feel he's a failure at *nine,* stinks.

[KEVIN *slams the phone down and turns back to*
BRONWEN.]

He's a great kid but he never stops asking questions. By the
time you've explained what a magistrate is you've missed
the whole bloody item.

BRONWEN: Look at this piece in a column from last week's
paper. Big businessman rumoured to have drawn out
huge amount of cash.

KEVIN: So?

BRONWEN: A lot of cash means something odd is going on,
doesn't it?

KEVIN: It can.

BRONWEN: Can I chase it up?

KEVIN: Waste of time. Believe me, Bronwen, I've been in this
business thirty years.

[BRONWEN *stares at the wall.*]

Bronnie, go and do sunshine or preservatives — take your
choice. Crystal's done a piece on workforce discrimination
and Nicole's done a piece on waiters. When something exciting comes in, I'll put you on to it.

[BRONWEN *continues to stare at the wall.*]

[*Screaming*] Bronnie, go and do skin cancer.

[*She retreats to her desk.* CRYSTAL *enters* KEVIN's *office
brandishing a print-out.*]

CRYSTAL: I know why you don't like it. You don't like what
it's saying.

KEVIN: I don't like it because I don't understand it. I have
a rule that I don't publish things I don't *understand.*

CRYSTAL: What's so difficult about it?

KEVIN: It's too abstract. You're telling us about women being
discriminated against in the workforce and there's not *one*
concrete example.

CRYSTAL: You can't draw conclusions from one example.

KEVIN: Stuff conclusions. Make us *feel* something. Find
someone who's been treated like shit and put us through
the same agony she suffered. Open a vein. Give us blood.

CRYSTAL: Yes, but . . .

KEVIN: Make us squirm. You'll do far more for your cause that way than all this bogus academic objectivity.

CRYSTAL: Where do I find someone who's been got at?

KEVIN: [*incredulous*] Go to an office tower, stand outside the lift and wait for a weeping woman to emerge.

CRYSTAL: Kevin . . .

KEVIN: Or even better — ring the PR guy of all the big companies and ask for a list of the women they've been treating like shit.

CRYSTAL: Very funny.

KEVIN: I don't give a stuff what you do, just make sure it's good enough to make me squirm!

[KEVIN *walks out of his office.*]

CRYSTAL: It'll be a pleasure.

[KEVIN *approaches* NICOLE.]

KEVIN: That was a good piece on waiters.

NICOLE: The sub cut my two best pars without even consulting me.

KEVIN: You really made those waiters come alive — which is more than I can say for the waiters who serve me.

NICOLE: Kevin, I want you to talk to the sub.

KEVIN: I cut 'em.

NICOLE: You cut them?

KEVIN: They were repetitive.

NICOLE: Has it ever occurred to you, Kevin, that writing is not just a matter of stuffing information down readers' throats? There is this indefinable thing, thought to be important by many, called style. Those pars were there for mood and atmosphere.

KEVIN: I tried to find you but you weren't around.

NICOLE: I was here all day.

KEVIN: Nicole, despite the fact that some people in the business call me the last of the macho illiterates, I know when paragraphs are redundant.

NICOLE: Next time, could you please consult me before you cut them?

KEVIN: You weren't around.

NICOLE: I was.

KEVIN: Nicole, I've got more important things to do than worry about your paragraphs.

NICOLE: Kevin, any professional journalist is concerned to see their work published at its best. If you don't think that's important —

KEVIN: Yes, it's important.

[*Pause.*]

Nothing's coming in on corruption and I'm getting edgy.

NICOLE: You can't expect loyalty from your staff if you're going to hack their work around.

KEVIN: Fair enough, Nicole, point taken!

[NICOLE *exits.*]

SCENE TEN

Some time later. KEVIN *is about to leave after a frustrating day. He is almost out of the building when the phone rings. There is a pause. Finally, he rushes back and picks it up. He listens.*

KEVIN: Who is this? Hang on, just wait till I get a pencil.

[*He scrabbles frantically on the desk.*]

Or a pen. Or even a scrap of paper.

[*He finds a lipstick on one of the desktops. He rolls up a trouser-leg and writes with the lipstick on his leg.*]

Go ahead. I'm listening.

[*Pause.*]

Nine months and he was in for nine years? What's his name? Your name?

[*The caller has obviously hung up.*]

Thanks, anyway.

[*He hangs up, looks at his leg, and hobbles off, holding his trouser leg.*]

SCENE ELEVEN

REX *is talking to* NICOLE *in a restaurant.*

REX: I suppose you guessed there might be more to this than a lunch?

NICOLE: It had crossed my mind.

REX: Now that you're working for the old firm again I thought we should clear up a few misunderstandings about the past. I don't regret our affair for a second but I really wish it hadn't happened.

NICOLE: There seems to be an inconsistency in there somewhere.

REX: I was a boss and that sort of thing lays itself open to misinterpretation.

NICOLE: In what way?

REX: It can have the appearance of sexual harassment — in our case I'm sure it wasn't.

   [*Pause.*]

   It's only harassment if the advances are unwelcome.

   [*Pause.*]

   I just wanted to assure you that my firing you had *nothing* to do with the fact that you became involved with someone else.

NICOLE: Good. I had wondered.

REX: Absolutely *nothing* to do with it.

NICOLE: Can you tell me what it *was* to do with?

REX: Cost-cutting. Pure and simple.

NICOLE: Why was I singled out?

REX: There did seem to be some tension developing.

NICOLE: Due to me?

REX: I think some of the men were having problems about a woman writing on the economy.

NICOLE: Why can't some men accept that women might be their intellectual equals?

REX: It's a mystery to me.

   [*Pause.*]

   I hope there are no hard feelings.

NICOLE: I wasn't delighted when it happened.
REX: No.
> [*Pause.*]

I was surprised you took the job.
NICOLE: I've been applying for anything that would get me out of the *Mail* for the last two years.
REX: Not happy there?
NICOLE: I'd applied for the deputy editorship so many times it was getting embarrassing. If a man isn't ambitious he's a wimp, but if a woman is she's a scheming bitch.
REX: Nobody ever says that about you.
> [*Pause.*]

What do you think of Kevin's other appointments?
NICOLE: Crystal must be intelligent.
REX: Have you read some of the stuff she used to write in her journal?
NICOLE: No, but anyone who can keep up with the changes in feminist ideology *must* have an agile brain.
REX: What about the other one?
NICOLE: Hard to say, she never talks.
REX: I hope Kevin knows what he's doing.
NICOLE: Kevin's appointment raised a lot of eyebrows.
REX: Why?
NICOLE: The consensus is he's past his peak — but then you know him better than most. You're old friends.
REX: [*nervously*] I'm excited about the new editorial policy. There's a lot of disquiet about corruption out there — don't you think?
NICOLE: You're a lot closer to the pulse than I am.
REX: Don't you sense that people are fed up? They really want to know what's going on?
NICOLE: You could be right. But I suppose Warren's hoping it'll boost circulation.
REX: Sure. But I think the prime concern is that we don't want to live in a country that's rotting at the core.
> [*Pause.*]

You look dubious?
NICOLE: I don't want to live in a country that's rotting at the core, either. I'm just wondering how much impact one

newspaper can make.

REX: One newspaper got rid of Nixon.

NICOLE: Now we've got Reagan.

SCENE TWELVE

REX *and* KEVIN *enter a lift.*

REX: Have you got any idea who phoned you?

KEVIN: No. But I'm pretty sure. It was a cop.

REX: Why?

KEVIN: Tone of voice and motive.

REX: What's the motive?

KEVIN: Frustration. They put in a lot of work, get the guy sent to prison for nine years and he's out again in nine months.

REX: They let everyone out early these days.

KEVIN: Not that early. He had a non-parole period of four years. He was released on the personal recommendation of the Minister for Justice.

REX: And the guy let out was convicted of . . .

KEVIN: Heroin trafficking. He organises couriers for Ray Rice.

REX: Where is he now?

KEVIN: Gone. Out of the country, on a false passport. He's probably back on the job in Thailand — buying stuff and organising couriers to bring it back into the country.

REX: [*shaking his head*] I can't wear it, mate.

KEVIN: Have you any idea the amount of money involved in a big heroin operation? They can afford to buy off whoever they like.

REX: Yes, but a Cabinet Minister?

KEVIN: Remember Terry Clark? He had customs agents, top cops and God knows who else on the payroll.

REX: It does sound a bit on the nose but for Christ's sake find out a hell of a lot more before you print anything.

KEVIN: I intend to.

REX: Ministers of the Crown getting drug money — that's

minefield journalism. One false step and you're history.

KEVIN: I'm a careful man, Rex.

REX: You've made mistakes before. Manila envelope?

KEVIN: I was set up by Rice. I won't make the same mistake again.

REX: Find out a hell of a lot more before you print anything.

SCENE THIRTEEN

KEVIN's *office. A projection of a cautious front page lay-out appears on the screen. He screams 'No!' as he sees it. It changes to a cover featuring his corrupt Minister/drug courier story. He utters a satisfied 'Yes'.*

SCENE FOURTEEN

WARREN BELCONNEN's *office. He is pacing around and he is not happy.* REX *enters, followed by* KEVIN. WARREN *turns and stares at* KEVIN.

WARREN: Kevin, I've had Gary Quest roaring at me on the phone half the morning.

KEVIN: Good, he's worried.

WARREN: What kind of smart arse reply is that?

REX: Kevin, I made it absolutely clear you weren't to publish about this till we were many more kilometres down the track.

KEVIN: Sometimes you have to fly a kite to get things started.

WARREN: Fly a kite? You've put an electric billboard up there and it's flashing 'Sue the arse off Warren Belconnen'.

REX: [*reading from paper*] 'People are asking why the Minister for Justice . . ."

KEVIN: People *are* asking it. I'm people, I'm asking.

WARREN: [*to* KEVIN) They told me you were a trouble maker. You're fired.

KEVIN: I've got a bloody contract.

WARREN: And I've got lawyers that warm up on contracts three times as tough as yours.

REX: Warren had a right to know what you were planning to do.

WARREN: I find it *totally* unbelievable that Ray Rice had Cabinet Ministers on his payroll.

REX: There's no way we could *prove* it even if it was true.

WARREN: I'm a personal friend of Gary Quest's. I had lunch with him two days ago. As far as I'm concerned he's been an effective and competent premier of this State and I won't have him condemned by innuendo and gossip.

KEVIN: I'm not condemning Quest, I'm asking questions about his Justice Minister, Costello.

WARREN: And you don't think that's going to hurt Quest? Where do you live? Fairyland?

KEVIN: It's not my business to worry about who's hurt and who isn't.

WARREN: What *is* your business?

KEVIN: To print the facts and the facts are that the key drug runner in Ray Rice's operation was let out of prison eight years early. That's everyone's business.

WARREN: There are dozens of other explanations.

KEVIN: Such as?

REX: Maybe he has genuinely reformed.

KEVIN: [*to* WARREN *indicating* REX] *There's* your refugee from Fairyland.

WARREN: Have you got any proof that Costello took money from Rice?

KEVIN: Of course I haven't.

WARREN: Rex has my full authority to decide what's printed and what isn't and he must *not* be bypassed.

REX: We've put you into one of the most sensitive jobs in the country, Kevin. There's no room for your old 'shoot from the hip' style in this sort of exercise.

WARREN: Understood?

SCENE FIFTEEN

Centre corridor. KEVIN *bashes a rolled-up paper on his leg.*

SCENE SIXTEEN

A hotel bar. KEVIN *is talking to* LAURIE BYRNE.

LAURIE: I'm out of the Force, Kev. I can't give you anything that's much use any more.

KEVIN: You're still in touch, Laurie.

LAURIE: I gave you stuff for years, mate, what good did it do?

KEVIN: Made a lot of people more careful.

LAURIE: How many convictions?

KEVIN: Plenty. A few . . .

[*Pause.*]

Three.

LAURIE: Three.

KEVIN: Costello let out one of Ray Rice's boys eight years early.

LAURIE: And was quite a bit wealthier after he'd done it.

KEVIN: You know about it?

LAURIE: Everyone in the crime unit knows it.

KEVIN: How?

LAURIE: They've got a tape of Rice's lawyer setting up the deal.

KEVIN: Speaking to Costello directly?

LAURIE: Yep. It's one of the more popular tapes down there at the moment. They play it when they want to whip themselves into a fury before a drug bust. Better than the theme from *Rocky*.

KEVIN: Laurie, when guys we elect start working for Race Rice then it's time to go for broke.

LAURIE: How?

KEVIN: Get me a copy of that tape and I'll publish it.

LAURIE: [*laughing*] Now pull the other leg.

KEVIN: I mean it — I'll fucking well publish it. How much longer do we have to sit round and watch it happen, Laurie?

LAURIE: You'd never get it printed.

KEVIN: You get me the tapes, I'll print them!

LAURIE: Belconnen's not going to let you print stuff like that.

KEVIN: You let me worry about that. How many times in the last ten years have you caught the big operators? I'm no moral crusader, Laurie, but someone's got to stop the pricks. [*Pause.*]

LAURIE: Don't bother booking a place in a retirement village if you take this one on, Kev old mate.

KEVIN: Can you imagine me in bowls gear? [*Pause.*]

LAURIE: It is a pretty gruesome thought.

SCENE SEVENTEEN

REX'*s office.* KEVIN *is reading* REX *the contents of a transcript.*

KEVIN: 'Costello: Tricky one, mate, I pulled his form out and he's in on possession and dealing. Lawyer: He was set up mate. They planted five kilos on him. Costello: Just can't spring someone who's involved in dealing. Lawyer: He works for Ray. Ray's not in the drug trade. Costello: It's a sticky one, mate. He's only been in nine months. Lawyer: Do your best — it's worth twenty. Ray sends his regards. He often thinks of the old days.'

REX: Twenty?

KEVIN: Twenty thousand dollars.

REX: Costello didn't want to let him out if he was involved with the drug trade.

KEVIN: He's out, and Costello is twenty thousand dollars richer.

REX: It's incredible. I wouldn't've believed it.

KEVIN: We've got to publish.

REX: If it's humanly possible we will.

KEVIN: Why wouldn't it be possible?

REX: You know what the libel laws are like.

KEVIN: Absolutely. They're there to make sure the rich, the powerful and the crooked stay rich, powerful and crooked.

REX: The libel suits on something like this would be over the moon. Massive.

KEVIN: Rex, we'd be printing words right out of the man's mouth. How can he sue?

REX: How do we prove the tapes are authentic?

KEVIN: They are. We can get voice prints done and prove it's their voices.

REX: This is going to rock the country to its foundations. This is Watergate type material.

KEVIN: Yep.

REX: It's death threat territory.

KEVIN: You wanted three a week.

REX: This is *real* death threat territory.

KEVIN: Travel to the office by a different route and watch your mail.

REX: Can they put a bomb in an ordinary letter?

KEVIN: Too right.

REX: How do you pick 'em?

KEVIN: They blow your arms off.

　　　[*They both laugh.*]

REX: Cut it out. I've got a wife and four kids.

KEVIN: This is what your life's been lacking, old mate. A touch of the knife edge.

REX: I'm serious. Once someone like Ray Rice knows we're on his trail —

KEVIN: They wouldn't dare touch you, mate. There'd be a massive backlash from all the journalists around the country who hold you in respect.

　　　[*Pause.*]

　　Might be better if you *didn't* open letters for a while.

REX: This is a big game to you. A schoolboy prank. Don't you realise the implications?

KEVIN: [*seriously*] I do.

　　　[*Pause.*]

REX: I'll have to clear this with Warren.

KEVIN: [*alarmed*] No you don't. This is your responsibility, mate. Don't go running to Warren.

REX: If the tapes were authenticated —

KEVIN: Rex, for the first time in my life I've got the goods on the boys at the top, and if you block this one I'll have a concrete job done on you and think it's the best value for money I've ever had.

REX: I want to publish this, Kevin, but the implications are enormous. This could bring down the government — or destroy us.

KEVIN: Listen, you great pile of dog turd, if there was one line of truth in that spiel you handed me about how you looked in the mirror and wanted to do something for your fellow man . . .

REX: I meant every word I said.

KEVIN: Then make the decision yourself. Don't go near the lawyers and don't run to Warren.

SCENE EIGHTEEN

The main office area. KEVIN *sits on a bench reading a print-out.* CRYSTAL *watches and waits nervously.*

KEVIN: [*reading*] 'She departed the meeting in a highly emotional state'?

CRYSTAL: She did.

KEVIN: Why not, 'She left the room in tears'?

CRYSTAL: [*shaking her head*] I'd rather keep it as it is.

KEVIN: Did she leave the room in tears?

CRYSTAL: Yes, but . . .

KEVIN: It's much simpler and more dramatic.

CRYSTAL: I don't want men to say, 'Ah yes, typical woman'.

KEVIN: [*reading*] 'The men started behaving like absolute shits the moment she was promoted above them. The amazing thing is that she didn't cry sooner'.

[*Pause.*]

OK, we'll leave it as it is.

[KEVIN *puts down the print-out and nods. He begins to move away.*]

CRYSTAL: [*nervously*] Is it OK?

KEVIN: Yep.

CRYSTAL: You going to run it?

KEVIN: Yep. Next week.

CRYSTAL: Was it — er — did it have the emotional impact you were after?

KEVIN: [*non-commitally*] Yeah.

CRYSTAL: Was it worse than you expected? Better than you expected? Did it make you squirm? I'd like a little bit of feedback.

KEVIN: If it had been lousy I would have told you.

CRYSTAL: I put weeks of work into that.

KEVIN: It was good.

CRYSTAL: Did it make you squirm?

KEVIN: It would've if I was a chauvinist.

CRYSTAL: What a joke.

KEVIN: You think I am?

CRYSTAL: Dead set.

KEVIN: [*hurt*] Why?

CRYSTAL: You spend most of your day drooling over eighteen-year-old typists.

KEVIN: Oh, is that a fact? Well, perhaps you'd like to read what I really do in my spare moments.

[*He gives her his latest article. She starts to read.*]

I've got about as much chance of getting one of our typists into bed as I have of reaching sixty. They're all tough little tarts called Lorraine who've made some monosyllabic hulk called Wes put a deposit on a quarter acre of blasted heath forty miles from anywhere in return for a hand job every Saturday night.

CRYSTAL: Sexist.

KEVIN: Wes told me!

CRYSTAL: Will they let you print this?

KEVIN: They better. Or I'm resigning!

CRYSTAL: [*disbelievingly*] A cabinet minister!

KEVIN: Money is money.

CRYSTAL: Makes my article seem a bit insignificant.

KEVIN: No, it's great, really.

[*He holds up his article.*]

You get one like this every ten years . . . if you're lucky.

CRYSTAL: You going to the pub?

KEVIN: Oh thanks, but I can't. My kid's a cat in the school concert.

CRYSTAL: Oh.

KEVIN: You've got one with you, haven't you?

CRYSTAL: What? A cat or a kid?

KEVIN: A child person.

CRYSTAL: Yeah. My girl.

KEVIN: Do you talk much to her?

CRYSTAL: Yeah, but I'm a talker.

KEVIN: Alan and I just seem to grunt at one another. What do you talk about?

CRYSTAL: She tells me all about her friends at school.

KEVIN: My little bugger makes me nervous. The Warren Belconnens of this world I can eat for breakfast but my own kid makes me nervous.

CRYSTAL: That's because you want your boy to like you. You don't care what Warren Belconnen thinks.

KEVIN: Could be. When did your old man leave?

CRYSTAL: Eighteen months ago.

KEVIN: Glad?

CRYSTAL: No. I was really depressed. He went off with a twenty-three-year-old.

KEVIN: Mine shot through with a youngie too. Got someone else?

CRYSTAL: The odd gentleman caller and when I say odd, I mean it. What about you?

KEVIN: No. Still, I'm not exactly your laughing cavalier.

CRYSTAL: You're OK.

KEVIN: Your average typist's not going to crawl over Mel Gibson to get to me. Right?

CRYSTAL: Don't put yourself down. You're verging on . . . sexy.

KEVIN: Hugh!

CRYSTAL: Bronwen thinks you're terrific.

[*Pause.*]

KEVIN: Has she said anything?

CRYSTAL: Not directly.

KEVIN: Yeah, well —

CRYSTAL: But I can tell.

KEVIN: No, it's a disaster if you get involved with someone you work with.

CRYSTAL: One of the subs told me you had a reputation as a womaniser.

[*Pause.*]

KEVIN: I had to lie a lot to get it.

[CRYSTAL *smiles and moves off. She reaches the door and turns back.*]

CRYSTAL: If they don't print it, I'll resign too.

SCENE NINETEEN

WARREN's *office.* KEVIN *faces* REX *and* WARREN.

REX: I'm sorry, Kevin, but I felt Warren had to be brought in on something as big as this.

KEVIN: What's the trouble, Mr Belconnen?

REX: Our lawyers are terrified.

KEVIN: Lawyers are always terrified. They're rabbits.

WARREN: [*to* KEVIN) Can you produce the makers of these tapes to swear in court to their authenticity?

KEVIN: No.

WARREN: Do you know who made the tapes?

KEVIN: No.

WARREN: Do you know who gave them to us?

KEVIN: Yes.

WARREN: Would you name him in court?

KEVIN: No.

REX: [*to* WARREN] You can see my problem.

WARREN: If you can't authenticate the tapes, you can't publish. What's the problem?

REX: The problem is I want to publish them. I'm fairly convinced the tapes are authentic.

WARREN: When you're *totally* convinced they're authentic —
publish. If you're not don't.

REX: There's a slight chance that they're fake.

KEVIN: Why would they be fake?

REX: Somebody might be out to get us.

KEVIN: I trust my source.

REX: You trusted your source once before.

KEVIN: Manila envelope. Manila envelope. Whenever anybody wants to spike me, out comes the old manila envelope.

REX: You've got to be absolutely sure.

KEVIN: I am sure.

REX: And even if we're sure we still can't prove they're authentic.

KEVIN: We can get voice prints done and prove it's their
voices.

REX: [*to* WARREN] I am almost totally convinced they're
authentic.

KEVIN: When you are totally convinced, publish.

REX: Warren, I felt out of courtesy you should be informed.
Quest is your friend.

WARREN: If one of his Ministers has been caught out, tough
luck for Quest. Some politicians think that friendship with
me guarantees them immortality, Quest isn't that stupid.
[*Pause.*]
And he's not that good a friend.

REX: This is sudden death territory, Warren. I appreciate you
giving me total responsibility for the *Review* but I thought
this was a decision you should make.

WARREN: Rex, I'm paying you a fortune to make this sort of
decision and cop the agonising that goes with it. Don't try
and transfer your ulcers to me.

REX: All right then, I'll publish.

WARREN: [*to his secretary, on a dictaphone*] Marjorie. Cancel
next week's lunch with Gary Quest.

REX: What if I'm wrong?

WARREN: What if you're wrong? I'll write you an excellent
reference.

SCENE TWENTY

The main office area. KEVIN, NICOLE, CRYSTAL *and* BRONWEN *sit watching the Premier,* GARY QUEST, *being interviewed on TV. As before, the head of* GARY QUEST *is projected onto a large screen.* RICHARD, *the interviewer, is off-screen.*

QUEST: I have spoken to Mr Costello and he assures me that the alleged conversation printed in the *Review* never took place.

RICHARD [*off*] He's certain of that?

QUEST: Absolutely. The allegation that one of my Ministers would accept money from an alleged drug dealer is not only preposterous, it's lunatic.

RICHARD: You don't think the tapes are authentic?

QUEST: Of course they're not authentic. Can they produce the person who made them? Of course they can't. Can they produce the person who gave them to them? No, not even that.

RICHARD: They say they're protecting their source.

QUEST: Oh yes, yes, how often have we heard that piece of journalistic clap trap. They protect some criminal selling them bogus tapes but they never give a second thought to besmirching the reputation of a hard-working and re-spected Minister of the Crown. As far as I'm concerned journalists who resort to this sort of tactic are no better than mangy ticks, burrowing for blood.

RICHARD: If the tapes aren't authentic, hasn't the *Review* laid itself open to a massive law suit?

QUEST: Too jolly right it has. And if I was Mr Costello. I'd show them no mercy.

RICHARD: Even if it forced the *Review* to close down?

QUEST: If Mr Costello caused the closure of the *Review,* he'd be doing the State a great public service. Men who have no hestitation descending into the stinking sewers of innu-endo are not the sort of men who should be given a voice in a free society.

[*There is a gloomy silence.*]

KEVIN: And ninety per cent of the population will believe every word he said.

[*A worried-looking* REX *approaches.*]

[*Sotto voce*] And speaking of mangy ticks . . .

REX: [*coming into earshot*] The writ's just come in.

KEVIN: How much for?

REX: Five million. It's a record.

[WARREN *enters and stares at* KEVIN.]

WARREN: I think . . . this calls for a drink.

[*He pulls a bottle of champagne from behind his back.*]

CRYSTAL: Bollinger!

WARREN: When you're down five million, what's an extra dollar or two?

CRYSTAL: What do we do now?

WARREN: We sit here and drink French champagne and hope to hell Kevin was right.

[WARREN *pours the drinks and offers a toast.*]

KEVIN: The truth!

WARREN: The truth — however embarrassing, inconvenient and . . . financially disastrous. The truth.

[*They raise their glasses. They all look more than slightly apprehensive.*]

END OF ACT ONE

ACT TWO

SCENE ONE

REX *is in his office.* KEVIN *stands by the window in his office reading.* REX *phones* KEVIN.

REX: Costello will withdraw the writ if we publish an apology and admit that the tapes are fake.

KEVIN: Tell him to get stuffed. He's beaten and he knows it.

REX: He doesn't exactly sound like a beaten man.

KEVIN: Do you think a hungry weasel like Costello would offer a truce if he thought he could go on and make an easy five million?

REX: If they take us to court, we can't authenticate the tapes.

KEVIN: We can have voice prints done and prove it's their voices. He's gone, Rex, and he knows it.

REX: Mate, I hope you're right.

SCENE TWO

The main office area. KEVIN, NICOLE, BRONWEN, CRYSTAL *and* REX *watch* GARY QUEST *being interviewed on TV.*

RICHARD: [*off*] The fact that you have suspended Mr Costello does seem to place *some* credence on the allegations.

QUEST: Come on now, Richard. You're an intelligent man. You know it places absolutely no credence on anything. It's simply that the smears and innuendoes have reached such a pitch that I feel the public trust in my administration can only be restored by a judicial enquiry, and until that enquiry is completed it is right and proper that Mr Costello step down.

RICHARD: Mr Costello has withdrawn his law suit against the Belconnen press.

QUEST: Mr Costello was forced to take out a writ to protect

his reputation. He is now confident that a judicial enquiry will achieve this end and that the writ is no longer required.

[*The journalists show what they think of this explanation — by giving it loud and derisive cat calls.* KEVIN *turns the set off. They are jubilant.*]

BRONWEN: Look, Kevin hasn't even managed a smile.

CRYSTAL: Come on, granite face, crack it.

[*He smiles. They applaud.*]

REX: I'd like to congratulate Kevin for striking one of the most significant blows for truth and decency in the history of this country. I'd like you to charge your glasses and drink a toast to someone who has emerged from the 'stinking sewers of innuendo' with his reputation untarnished and his actions vindicated. We drank Bollinger on the brink of disaster, we drink it again in triumph.

BRONWEN: I wonder what they're drinking in Quest's office.

CRYSTAL: Cyanide!

KEVIN: Bugger the Bollinger, let's go to the pub.

BRONWEN: And book it up to Belconnen.

KEVIN: He can afford it: he just saved five million.

[*They begin to exit.* CRYSTAL *glances at* NICOLE *and notices that she's not joining in. Her participation in the celebration is, at best, half-hearted.*]

CRYSTAL: [*to* NICOLE] Come on, snap out of it!

SCENE THREE

Some days later. CRYSTAL *and* NICOLE *sit in the office watching* KEVIN *being interviewed on television.*

RICHARD: [*off*] Are there more revelations to come?

KEVIN: We're working on it.

RICHARD: Are you pursuing a vendetta against the Quest Government?

KEVIN: That's a very provocative way to ask a question, Richard. I'm pursuing what journalists are paid to pursue. The truth. You should try it sometime.

[*He laughs.*]

RICHARD: You don't think you might have bitten off more than you can chew?

KEVIN: Gary Quest is a citizen like anyone else. We found evidence of corruption in his ministry and we'll look for more. If there isn't any more, then he's got nothing to worry about, has he?

RICHARD: Have you got anything to worry about, Kevin?

KEVIN: My conscience is clear.

NICOLE: Loves it.

CRYSTAL: Who?

NICOLE: Kevin. Loves the publicity.

CRYSTAL: He's only human.

NICOLE: Wants everyone to know that he's the man who put a dent in the great Gary Quest.

CRYSTAL: Got to allow him a bit of ego. Quest never had to duck for cover like this before.

NICOLE: I'm not at all sure we should be so delighted.

CRYSTAL: I am. One of his Ministers has —

NICOLE: I know what one of his Ministers has done. The other side of the coin is that Quest's government has instigated the most important social reforms this State's ever had.

SCENE FOUR

WARREN's *office.* WARREN *is about to commence a bit of wine tasting.* REX *enters.*

REX: Circulation's up by four thousand.

WARREN: Satisfied?

REX: I thought it might have been more, but at least the tide has turned.

WARREN: Try some of this. A friend of mine, Jason Ingles, keeps sending me the bloody stuff.

REX: Barossa?

WARREN: Queensland.

[*Pause.*]

REX: Nice wine.

WARREN: It's shit.

REX: Did you see the polls? Quest's popularity has taken a nose dive.

WARREN: He's got to expect it.

REX: Do you think Quest's clean?

WARREN: Yes . . . except for the usual perks.

REX: What's he on to?

WARREN: A fairly dubious tax scheme that I put him on to.

REX: Really?

WARREN: And half shares in a vineyard with Jason Ingles.

REX: A gift?

WARREN: Not technically. A loan that he repays over fifty years.

REX: Why would Ingles give Quest a vineyard?

WARREN: He thought it might help to have the Premier on side when Cabinet was discussing one of his development 'projects'.

REX: Has it helped?

WARREN: [*part humorously*] No. It's not Quest who's the problem. It's his Ministers.

REX: Yes. Most of them look as though they started their careers as hit men.

WARREN: Exactly. Quest was brought in as window dressing. The Labor Party in this State is still in the hands of Tammany Hall thugs.

REX: [*nodding*] Street boys.

WARREN: The Ray Rices and the Costellos went to school together. Half of them chose crime, the other half chose politics, and there's always been a fairly fluid interchange between the two.

REX: [*nodding*] You take a minor union official with no ex-

perience other than rigging elections and suddenly make
him Minister for whatever . . .

WARREN: And it's like putting a kid in a toy shop with no one
watching.

REX: There have been some good Labor governments, of
course.

WARREN: I must have missed them.

REX: Curtin, Chifley —

WARREN: Barely adequate.

REX: And Quest's brought in some long overdue reforms.

WARREN: Gary Quest has made this State a paradise for gays,
lesbians, feminists and bludgers, but he hasn't made much
of a fist of running things.

REX: I thought he was your friend?

WARREN: You don't have friends in our business, Rex.
Aquaintances and allies. I won't be sorry to see Quest go.

REX: I'm not so sure about that.

WARREN: You've got an endearing attachment to adolescent
dreams of equality and fraternity, Rex. The Labor Party is
the losers' party. If you end up on the bottom of the heap,
you blame the system.

REX: A society isn't up to much if it hasn't got compassion
for its underdogs.

WARREN: Let them organise it for themselves.

   [*Pause.*]

Don't look at me as if I'm Attila the Hun. I don't want us
to cancel the dole and go back to soup kitchens.

   [*Pause.*]

Quest feels no more warmly about me than I do about him,
I can assure you. You should know by now, Rex, that on
the top rungs of the ladder of power the word 'friend' just
doesn't apply.

   [*He gives him the carton of wine.*]

There's just acquaintances and allies.

SCENE FIVE

The main office area. NICOLE *is at her video display terminal.* CRYSTAL *enters.*

CRYSTAL: This city is so full of gays you're liable to end up a lesbian by default.

NICOLE: What prompted that?

CRYSTAL: I went out last night hoping to bump into something tall, dark and exciting. Hm!

NICOLE: No?

CRYSTAL: I only had one offer all night!

NICOLE: Not your type?

CRYSTAL: He had nice hair . . . it just would have looked better on somebody else.

NICOLE: Sounds like a great night out.

CRYSTAL: How are you making out?

NICOLE: The minute I find a rich, genial bachelor I'll marry him. I've proved I can be independent but enough's enough.

CRYSTAL: You'd stop working?

NICOLE: Faster than a speeding bullet.

CRYSTAL: And play tennis and drink coffee?

NICOLE: And lie in the sun and read and travel and eat in the best restaurants and swim in my pool and maybe even have a baby. I'm sick of lying awake at night worrying about meeting a deadline and whether the work will be good enough when I do!

CRYSTAL: I've been married. It stinks!

NICOLE: Was he genial and wealthy?

CRYSTAL [*shaking her head*] Mean and nasty.

NICOLE: That's the difference.

CRYSTAL: Where are you going to get this amazing spouse?

NICOLE: That's my problem.

[REX *goes past looking suave, sophisticated and totally aware of it. He nods and smiles at them as he passes.*]

Has God's gift propositioned you yet?

CRYSTAL: No.

NICOLE: He will.

> [BRONWEN *appears at the far end of the office area and enters* KEVIN'S *office.*]

Here comes Tinkerbell.

CRYSTAL: Not exactly a bundle of laughs, is she?

NICOLE: You could say that.

CRYSTAL: I told Kevin that she had the hots for him.

NICOLE: Has she?

CRYSTAL: I don't know. I thought it might liven the place up. Don't you think they'd be 'good' for each other?

NICOLE: [*shaking her head*] Disaster.

> [BRONWEN, *looking intense and serious, moves towards her display terminal.*]

BRONWEN: Did you see Quest on television last night? He's starting to crack.

NICOLE: Lengthwise or ear to ear?

BRONWEN: [*ignoring her*] He didn't answer the questions, he just abused the interviewer.

CRYSTAL: Sounds like he's really rattled.

BRONWEN: He is. He's going to lose the next election.

NICOLE: Is that good?

BRONWEN: His cabinet's corrupt.

NICOLE: One of his ministers is corrupt.

BRONWEN: Two.

CRYSTAL: Two?

BRONWEN: Some big developers have been putting money into a special slush fund, and guess where it's been ending up?

NICOLE: Where did you hear this?

BRONWEN: One of the developers got fed up and talked.

NICOLE: Is that what you're working on now?

BRONWEN: [*nodding*] Kevin asked me to do this story.

> [NICOLE *looks at* CRYSTAL. *She is furious.*]

NICOLE: Any particular reason it was given to you?

BRONWEN: Kevin thought I could handle it.

CRYSTAL: This is really going to put Quest on the skids.

BRONWEN: He's finished. And good riddance too.

NICOLE: I know corruption is an obsession with this paper but forget about that for just a second and look at what Quest has done. We've got anti-discrimination and equal opportunity laws that have got teeth; day care centres, women's refuges and rape crisis centres —

BRONWEN: We've also got the country's biggest drug trade problem.

NICOLE: [*unfazed*] Public housing has tripled, ethnic minorities get special teaching in our schools at last. Four more national parks have been proclaimed in the last year.

BRONWEN: That doesn't excuse —

NICOLE: Thanks to Gary Quest we've got a State in which someone who isn't your standard mum with three kids can feel as if they're not a freak. Quite frankly, I couldn't give a damn if Gary Quest is sucked off every Saturday night by teenage nymphets in orgies run by Ray Rice. Quest has made this State one I can tolerate living in and I can't say that for many other places in the world. What exactly do you want, Bronwen? You want this State handed back to the people who sent decoy cops into public toilets to flush out the sodomites?

CRYSTAL: And put unionists in gaol and fine them a thousand dollars a day for going on strike?

BRONWEN: Quest's government is corrupt.

NICOLE: Bronwen, ever since the Rum Corps it's been assumed that the only reason anyone seeks public office in this country is to line their pockets.

BRONWEN: Corruption is like a cancer, Nicole. It spreads and in the end everyone pays.

NICOLE: Nonsense. It's no worse now than it was.

BRONWEN: Do you know how many teenagers are addicted to heroin in this State? Do you know what their life expectancy is?

NICOLE: Drugs are a problem —

BRONWEN: Do you think a drug trade the size of ours could operate without massive corruption?

NICOLE: Drugs are a problem but let's see it in perspective.

BRONWEN: That's a little hard if you've seen what I've seen.

NICOLE: Bronwen, I've been to all the sleaze pits —

BRONWEN: Then how can you put it in perspective?

NICOLE: Bronwen, I've been a journalist for nearly twenty years. I've been to every sleaze joint in the city and I've done my quota of articles on the broken and shattered lives of the young victims. But the sorry truth is, and I've never dared print this, because the liberal humanist dogma that dominates this society is that nobody is to blame for anything — we're all victims of a cruel and materialist society. The sorry truth is that most of those kids took to drugs because they were pretty limited human beings to begin with.

BRONWEN: That's a bit callous, isn't it?

NICOLE: It's the truth. I've seen them. I've spoken to them. The vast majority of kids who go on drugs are intellectually dull or emotionally unstable.

BRONWEN: So we just let them die?

NICOLE: Three thousand people a year are killed on the roads. Do we outlaw cars?

CRYSTAL: I think there's a difference.

NICOLE: I've got a nightmare vision of spending the rest of my life on an eternal round of interviews with ex-policemen, petty crims, shady businessmen and corrupt lawyers on a holy crusade to rid ourselves of something we'll never rid ourselves of for the sake of a few thousand gormless kids who can't handle the pressures of life.

BRONWEN: [rising] Why don't you go and work on a fashion magazine? It's more your style.

[BRONWEN storms off.]

NICOLE: I can't stand moral zealots.

CRYSTAL: I noticed.

[She busies herself with her word processor.]

SCENE SIX

KEVIN's office. KEVIN enters wearing a new suit. NICOLE and CRYSTAL cannot believe this new 'media image'. BRONWEN enters.

BRONWEN: Kevin.

KEVIN: Yes, Bronnie.

BRONWEN: I traced that cash.

KEVIN: What cash?

BRONWEN: The news item about the businessman who'd drawn out a lot of cash.

KEVIN: Oh, that.

BRONWEN: It was a guy called Jason Ingles. He's into vineyards and property development. Know him?

KEVIN: He's not in the big league. He's wealthy but he's not a Murdoch or a Packer.

BRONWEN: He took out half a million.

KEVIN: [*raising his eyebrows*] How did you find that out?

BRONWEN: I went to the bank and told the manager I was doing an article on stress management. I got talking to this young teller who fancied himself. He couldn't wait to tell me about the day he handled half a million in cash. 'Made the papers' he said proudly.

KEVIN: And he told you it was Ingles?

BRONWEN: [*blushing*] Eventually.

KEVIN: You didn't compromise your honour, I hope?

BRONWEN: I had to — you know —
    [*Pause.*]

KEVIN: No, I don't know. Please tell me.

BRONWEN: Have a few drinks and all that.

KEVIN: All what?

BRONWEN: Listen to his records. At least he had a good rock collection.

KEVIN: You're a regular Mata Hari.

BRONWEN: I didn't do anything I didn't enjoy.

KEVIN: I don't think I want to hear this.

BRONWEN: There's nothing to hear.
    [*There is a pause.*]

KEVIN: Half a million, you say?

BRONWEN: Why would he want that much in cash?

KEVIN: A cheque can always be traced.

BRONWEN: Where do you think it was going?

KEVIN: If it's Ingles I'm pretty sure it's not drugs.

BRONWEN: Why couldn't it be drugs?

KEVIN: I'd believe Jesus was a card sharp if I heard it from the right source but Ingles is Establishment, squeaky clean. His wife works the charity circuit.

BRONWEN: He seemed very nervous when I put it to him.

KEVIN: [*anxiously*] Put it to him? Put what to him?

BRONWEN: Why he'd drawn out half a million in cash.

KEVIN: Jesus, Bronnie, did it ever occur to you that it might have been a bit premature to go and front him? What did he say?

BRONWEN: He denied it.

KEVIN: I bet he did.

BRONWEN: Can we run it?

KEVIN: Run what?

BRONWEN: That he drew out half a million in cash.

KEVIN: It's unusual but it's not a crime.

BRONWEN: We could say that this sort of cash withdrawal is normally associated with drugs.

KEVIN: [*sarcastically*] That would be a clever move except that there's this thing called libel.

BRONWEN: We're not saying he used it for drugs.

KEVIN: But we're implying. The libel laws state that you can't even *hint* at anything nasty about someone whose home has appeared in *House and Garden,* and the Ingles have had theirs in twice. Bronnie, I'm impressed with your initiative — dubious about your methods but certainly impressed with your initiative. However, in future let's plan our strategy together, hmm?

BRONWEN: The label's still on your sleeve.

[*She exits.*]

SCENE SEVEN

The main office area. REX *enters and looks around.* CRYSTAL *is there working at her machine.* REX *looks around ignoring* KEVIN's *new disguise.*

REX: [*smiling*] Seen Kevin?

CRYSTAL: No.

REX: We must get together for lunch.

CRYSTAL: Oh, right.

[CRYSTAL *makes a fast exit.*]

REX: [*indicating a suitcase*] More tapes?

KEVIN: No: transcripts.

REX: Got a second?

KEVIN: Come in.

[REX *is already in. He takes a seat.*]

Take a seat.

REX: Warren got a call from Jason Ingles, a businessman into property development and vineyards.

KEVIN: I know him.

REX: Warren went to school with him.

KEVIN: Well, I guess they've got a lot to chat about. Who was up who in the dorm after lights out — all that sort of stuff.

REX: Young Bronwen apparently went to see him and made some bizarre accusations.

KEVIN: I sent her.

REX: Something about a large sum of cash.

KEVIN: I heard a rumour that he'd drawn out half a million.

REX: He denies it categorically.

KEVIN: [*shrugging*] It was only a rumour. I hear hundreds.

REX: Why did you send Bronwen to see him?

KEVIN: She wanted something to do. You know how these youngies are, Rex. Ever since Bernstein and Woodpile they all want to be investigative.

REX: You had no evidence other than a rumour?

KEVIN: None at all.

REX: [*angrily*] I really wonder about you, Kevin. You're given the chance to make a real impact and you go out of your way to be deliberately irresponsible. Why?

KEVIN: Because you look so beautiful when you're angry.

REX: Don't get too cocky, circulation's down below what it was when you took over.

KEVIN: We've lost the wine and Mercedes lot.

REX: And we've lost the advertising that goes with it. It's not just the circulation drop, Kevin; firms like their ads placed in the right advertising environment.

KEVIN: Right environment?

REX: If you've got an up-market product you don't put it next to an article about drug use amongst prostitutes. We're losing circulation and advertising and it's starting to look serious.

KEVIN: Mate, you didn't bring me here to create the right advertising environment for underarm deodorants.

REX: This is a commercial world, Kevin. We've got to live with commercial reality —

KEVIN: Mate, you brought me here because you looked at yourself in the mirror one day and wanted to make this a better country.

REX: And I still do —

KEVIN: And we're doing it.

REX: It's not translating into readership.

KEVIN: Stuff readership. We're getting rid of corruption.

REX: All I want is a little variety.

KEVIN: We're not having those bloody wine supplements back again.

REX: I'm not just talking about —

KEVIN: The fact that seventy-eight Cabernet has attained an episcopal purple, might send shivers of delight down your spine but it doesn't do much for me.

REX: Corruption doesn't turn some readers on. I find it hard to wade through those transcripts myself.

KEVIN: Mate, those transcripts are spelling out the basic mechanics of corruption in this State.

REX: It can still make dull reading.

KEVIN: What would you rather read about? Some trendy twit getting rave reviews for his underwear designs in Paris?

REX: Mate, while you're out there tilting at windmills, I have to face the accountants.

KEVIN: I think you'd better go and take another look in that mirror of yours.

REX: Don't be so bloody arrogant, Kevin. I took you off the scrap heap and gave you one of the top jobs going.

KEVIN: Scrap heap? I was a top political journalist in Canberra.

REX: Like I said, I took you off the scrap heap and by Christ

I had to fight to get you appointed. Don't have any illusions about that.

KEVIN: What are you carrying on about? I've delivered.

REX: You haven't delivered circulation.

KEVIN: Stuff circulation.

REX: Don't you know the realities here, Kevin? Warren doesn't give a stuff about the *Review*. If it starts losing money consistently, he'll close it.

KEVIN: Bullshit. It's his most prestigious journal.

REX: Kevin, you might be hot on corruption but you don't know anything about power. As far as Warren's concerned the *Review* is a bad smell that hangs around him like dog shit on his shoes. The people he mixes with loathe it. They keep asking him why he allows such a grotty little scandal sheet to be published.

KEVIN: Why does he?

REX: [*suddenly angry*] Because of me! If I wasn't around here it would have closed years ago.

KEVIN: Bullshit.

REX: Of all the arseholes that ever lost the ability to compromise in some rap-knuckle parish classroom, you would have to be the most odious. If the *Review* folds be prepared to accept a *little* of the blame.

[*He exits.* BRONWEN *enters.*]

KEVIN: [*handing* BRONWEN *a transcript*] Here's something that might get us a bit closer. A big-spending car dealer called, would you believe, Terry Crook, phoning our crooked lawyer friend and asking him to help get a syndicate together.

BRONWEN: A drug syndicate?

KEVIN: They don't say as much but I don't think they're buying cabbages.

BRONWEN: Well, I've found out that Jason Ingles is in financial trouble.

KEVIN: What?

BRONWEN: Two of his vineyards were wiped out by hail and he's still trying to offload the tower blocks he built in Surfers Paradise.

KEVIN: Yeah?

BRONWEN: He sold his paintings a month ago and got almost half a million for them. That's obviously where he got the half million he drew out of the bank.

KEVIN: You're kidding!

BRONWEN: No, and there's a possible connection between Ingles and Gary Quest.

KEVIN: Quest?

BRONWEN: There's a rumour round that they're in a vineyard venture together.

KEVIN: Bronnie, track down the directors of every company involved in a partnership with Ingles.

BRONWEN: [*nodding*] I've started it already.

[*She turns to go.*]

KEVIN: Still seeing your bank teller?

BRONWEN: No.

KEVIN: One night stand?

BRONWEN: Very definitely.

KEVIN: Use them up and spit 'em out.

BRONWEN: That's right.

KEVIN: I'm here to be used.

BRONWEN: I'll keep it in mind.

[BRONWEN *smiles to herself and goes.*]

SCENE EIGHT

An up-market restaurant. REX *and* NICOLE *are finishing lunch.*

REX: I suppose you guessed that there might be more to this than a lunch?

NICOLE: Circulation's down again?

REX: Right.

NICOLE: It's scarcely surprising.

REX: It is to me. The transcripts we're printing are spelling out the basic mechanics of corruption in our society.

NICOLE: Everyone knows that corruption exists. They just don't want to hear about it. They want life to be like a breakfast food ad: happy kids on summer mornings. They want to believe that the world is basically nice, not a place where African kids starve and politicians lie and the rich and powerful rob and cheat. We're asking them to pay a dollar and a ꞏalf a week to be made uneasy about things they'd rather not know about.

[*Pause.*]

There was a newspaper strike in Milwaukee or somewhere once and the suicide rate dropped by half.

[*Pause.*]

Newspapers are bad-news-papers and our news is the baddest of them all.

REX: It is, isn't it?

NICOLE: We're into slash-your-wrists territory at the moment. Free blade with every copy.

REX: I don't want to step back from what Kevin's started. It's too important.

[NICOLE *gives a 'this way, that way' hand gesture.*]

You don't agree?

NICOLE: Crooked chicken franchises?

REX: All I want Kevin to do is broaden his scope. And I thought . . .

NICOLE: Some chance.

REX: If you were to talk to him . . .

NICOLE: He wouldn't listen.

REX: I must say I didn't get a reasoned response when I broached the matter.

NICOLE: He's obsessed.

REX: And if you don't *totally* share that obsession, you're held to be contemptible.

NICOLE: Utterly.

[*Pause.*]

REX: Nicole, if there is a blow up — and I'm hoping like hell there won't be — I'd like to know if you'd be prepared to take on Kevin's job.

[*There is a pause.* NICOLE *taps her fingers.*]

I respect Kevin for what he believes in . . .

NICOLE: So do I. But he's killing the paper.

SCENE NINE

The main office area. NICOLE, CRYSTAL *and* BRONWEN *are at their terminals.* KEVIN *enters.*

KEVIN: I've received a directive from upper management. It is written on paper, there are copies of it. It has a date and it's signed by Rex. Apparently, it is meant to be taken seriously.
  [*He reads it.*]
'The proprietor and I would like you to attempt to appeal to a broader target audience than you are at present. A group has been identified by American research and given the name Young Upwardly Mobile Professional Persons — or Yuppies. They are dedicated, fast track, male and female middle managers and professionals in their early twenties to early forties. Their lifestyle is a constant search for excellence and prestige in everything they do and acquire. Cars, restaurants, holidays, wine, books, collectibles, plays, travel, music and opera — all have to be the very best available within their price range. And their price range is high. The disposable income of Yuppie couples is often in the vicinity of a hundred thousand dollars. They tend to delay, or postpone indefinitely, having children. They are conservative on most issues, demanding cuts in tax and expressing little concern for the elderly or the poor. But they do express concern over nuclear war.'
  [*He looks up.*]
Presumably because they don't want their assets vaporised.
  [*He reads on.*]
'While not wanting to curtail your investigative function in any way, the proprietor and I would like articles of interest to this newly identified target to be written.' Signed, Rex Harding.
  [*Pause.*]
Well, I don't know about you but this lot sound like the

biggest bunch of deadshits I've ever heard of.

BRONWEN: If we start catering to them, we'll just become a consumer checklist for affluent narcissists.

KEVIN: Our readers might just as well buy *Vogue Living* and get the same stories on glossy paper.

[KEVIN *tears up the management directive.*]

CRYSTAL: I don't think you're being totally fair, Kevin.

BRONWEN: They don't care about the elderly, they don't care about the poor, all they care about is themselves. If we have to have best buys in nineteenth century porcelain, then I'm getting out.

NICOLE: Kevin, Rex's directive didn't ask you to stop your corruption probe.

BRONWEN: How can we keep it going at full steam if we've got to waste time and energy doing consumer shit?

CRYSTAL: I know the whole Yuppie thing can be made to sound appalling, but a lot of the ridicule directed at them is —

BRONWEN: Is because they deserve it.

CRYSTAL: Is because a lot of journos don't like the idea of career women. What's wrong with marrying someone who doesn't want you to have kids and turn you into a domestic?

NICOLE: And what's wrong with having an apartment with some decent furniture and paintings and a video hi-fi if you've got the energy and capacity to be earning at a level where you can afford it?

BRONWEN: If you never lift your eyes beyond your own career and your own selfish little consumer games in a world where three out of every four live in poverty, then I think you're worse than disgusting.

NICOLE: [*cool and tough*] Bronwen, if you want to take the world's inequities on your shoulders, you do it. But don't call people names because they're realistic enough to know that half their lives are gone and they aren't going to get another shot at inhabiting planet earth. If a 'fast track middle manager' in his forties offered to share his disposable income with mine right now, I'd jump at it. And the only reason I wouldn't delay my child is that I'm run-

ning out of time fast. If you think that makes me disgusting, then let me tell you what I think of you. You're a snot-
nosed little bigot riddled with a very common and in-
creasingly virulent disease called the arrogance of youth.

> [*The two women stare at each other.* KEVIN *breaks the ten-
> sion.*]

KEVIN: [*to* NICOLE] You'd be happy to write this sort of stuff
Rex wants?

NICOLE: Yes.

KEVIN: [*to* CRYSTAL] You too?

CRYSTAL: [*nervously*] I admire what you're doing Kevin, but
I would like to see a bit more space devoted to welfare and
women's issues.

KEVIN: We're not having the paper stuffed full of consumer
trends and bleeding heart feminism. Not as long as I'm
editor.

SCENE TEN

WARREN'*s office.* WARREN *sits.* REX *paces around.*

WARREN: [*calmly*] Sack him.

REX: Only as a last resort. He's a good journalist and an old
friend.

WARREN: I've no intention of continuing to subsidise the *Review* indefinitely, Rex. We're losing thousands a week.

REX: I asked him here to uncover the corruption and he's
done it. He's done it brilliantly. Better than I could have
done it or anyone else in the country. There's a lot of respect for him in the profession, Warren. He has achieved
something substantial.

WARREN: What? Undermined one grubby government so it
can be replaced by another? He can still publish his
bloody tapes as long as he stuffs them down the back and
puts something up front that people want to read.

REX: He won't do it.

WARREN: Then sack him. Look, Rex, I don't care if you print

Chinese couplets. All I want to see is sales go up.

REX: If I sacked him my name would be mud right through the profession.

WARREN: If I sack him my name'll be mud. No use coming to me, Rex, it's your problem, you handle it.

SCENE ELEVEN

KEVIN's *office.* KEVIN *and* BRONWEN *are reading transcripts.*

KEVIN: Bronnie. Listen to this. A conversation between our car dealer friend, Terry Crook, and our crooked lawyer. [*Reading*] 'Terry Crook: "Terry here, Bob." Lawyer: "Terry, how are you, mate? Just going to ring you. I've got you your man." Crook: "You're kidding. I was starting to get desperate." Lawyer: "Bloke I play golf with. He'll take up the whole half million." Crook: "Fabulous. When can I get it?" Lawyer: "In a week or two." Crook: "He knows it's got to be cash?" Lawyer: "Yep, he's selling his paintings to raise the dough." '

[BRONWEN *sits there stunned.*]

Our crooked lawyer and Ingles belong to the same golf club.

BRONWEN: We've got him.

[*Pause.*]

Will you get it published?

KEVIN: Try and stop me.

SCENE TWELVE

WARREN's *office.* KEVIN *and* REX *face* WARREN.

WARREN: It falls a long way short of proof.

KEVIN: Half a million. The paintings. His golfing mate. Come on, Warren, what sort of proof do you need?

REX: We wouldn't be making any allegations, Warren, we'd just be printing the tapes.

WARREN: We're implying that a respected businessman, who happens to be an old friend, is financing a drug operation. A businessman who's also in partnership with Gary Quest.

KEVIN: We're printing in the public interest what Terry Crook said to his mate.

WARREN: Ingles and I grew up together. There's no way he'd ever deal in drugs.

KEVIN: We're not saying he's dealing in drugs, he just wants half a million to buy something.

WARREN: You can't publish it.

KEVIN: Warren, there's no way you're going to stop this one.

WARREN: If I want to stop it, I'll stop it.

REX: The *Review* is *my* responsibility. You've made that more than clear on many occasions. We didn't come here to ask if we could publish, we came as a courtesy to let you know we were going to publish.

WARREN: Don't get legalistic with me, Rex. I own that paper and you aren't publishing.

REX: I can't accept that, Warren. Every other time you've made me take the sticky decisions and said that's what you pay me for.

WARREN: It's my paper.

REX: Warren, you've got to be consistent.

WARREN: I don't have to be anything. Don't publish this until I have a chance to think it through. Understood?

SCENE THIRTEEN

BRONWEN *is in the main office area. The phone rings, she answers and listens. She frowns, hangs up and goes to* KEVIN *in his office.*

KEVIN: What's wrong?

BRONWEN: I just got a call from some guy who said that if we publish the tape we're dead.

KEVIN: When? Just then?

[BRONWEN *nods.*]

What did he sound like?

BRONWEN: A real thug.

KEVIN: How the hell do they know? Did he ask for you by name?

BRONWEN: Yes.

KEVIN: How the fuck do they know?

SCENE FOURTEEN

WARREN'*s office.* KEVIN *and* REX *face each other.*

WARREN: Yes, I have talked to Jason. I felt I had to give him a chance to rebut.

KEVIN: Well, he's just talked to his friends and Bronnie and I have just got death threats.

WARREN: Death threats?

KEVIN: If you wanted any proof that he's got some pretty heavy friends then you've just got it.

REX: What did Ingles say?

WARREN: He said he didn't know it was heroin.

KEVIN: Well, what did he think it was? Stuffed parrots?

WARREN: Hash.

KEVIN: Oh, that's all right then if he thought it was only hash.

WARREN: I've had a five-hour session with him and he's shattered. He needed money in a hurry and he needed it desperately and they swore to him that it was hash. His whole business operation was about to go under.

KEVIN: Jeee-sus —

WARREN: I'm not making excuses for him. I gave him one hell of a serve. One hell of a serve. But he did it out of desperation, not greed.

KEVIN: Desperation is when you've got five kids to feed and no money. The worst Ingles was facing was selling off some assets.

WARREN: And letting the whole world know his business was on the skids.

REX: Warren, he made money on a drug deal. There's no question. We have to print the tape.

WARREN: He didn't do it out of greed. Rex, I know Jason. I know his wife. I know his children and I know what he's done for this country. He's a good, humane human being who must have been under enormous pressure to contemplate anything as crazy as this. Jason wasn't just thinking of his own skin, he's got a lot of employees depending on him. You lefties think that businessmen just sit back and enjoy their wealth without a care in the world.

KEVIN: I'm not a left-winger and I'm not a right-winger. My profession is to publish the facts and the fact is that your friend made a million dollars trading heroin.

REX: If there are any extenuating circumstances it's up to the courts to evaluate them, not us.

WARREN: Look, a sales rep came in here a few weeks ago and offered me a huge freight discount on our newsprint if we used his firm's containers. The only catch was that deliveries would take an extra half day to arrive here after they landed. I didn't have to be a genius to realise what was going on. It's happening all around us.

KEVIN: We're shifting ground here a little, aren't we? A few seconds ago he was doing it to save his workers' jobs, now he's innocently caught up in the heroin boom.

REX: Warren, be truthful. You're protecting an old mate and you're fishing for justifications.

WARREN: There's loyalty involved, yes.

REX: You told me there were no friendships in our game. Just acquaintances and alliances. I don't want to be sanctimonious, Warren, but we have to publish without fear or favour.

KEVIN: For years I've hoed into lefties who've told me our press is no more free than Russia's and what I've said to them is that our owners don't dictate what goes in. We do. What a joke.

WARREN: You've printed everything you've wanted to up to now.

KEVIN: That was OK. We were just destroying a Labor government.

WARREN: Politics doesn't enter into it.

KEVIN: Quest is just an upjumped boy from the wrong side of the tracks — not an old school mate.

REX: Warren, if we don't print that tape I'll have to resign.

WARREN: Could you send an old friend to prison?

KEVIN: I have.

WARREN: Then you're not much of a friend.

KEVIN: No, but I'm a bloody good journalist.

[Pause.]

WARREN: Nailing Ingles won't stop the heroin trade!

KEVIN: Have you ever had to interview the parents of a sixteen-year-old kid who's died of an overdose?

WARREN: Kevin —

KEVIN: When you have, you start to hate every greasy bastard that's connected with the whole stinking trade.

WARREN: Don't try that one on me, Kevin. You don't lose any sleep over the heroin trade, you only want your bloody story printed!

KEVIN: That's right. For thirty years I've worked stupid hours, eaten lousy food, chain-smoked and shortened my life by thirty years writing stories that were forgotten almost before they came off the press.

WARREN: Ingles is not a key figure in the heroin trade.

KEVIN: I couldn't give a stuff. He dealt in it.

REX: Are you still going to go up to him in the foyer on opening nights and shake his hand, Warren?

WARREN: Gary Quest's a partner with Jason Ingles in a vineyard. If that comes out he's finished. Do you know how difficult this government can make it for us if they really want to?

REX: They can't do much.

WARREN: They can use their union influence to get our newsprint and all our other supplies blackbanned. I've had Quest on the phone threatening me already.

KEVIN: And you're going to cave in without a fight?
   [*There is a long pause.*]
WARREN: [*to* REX] Publish it.
   [*Pause.*]
   For Christ's sake — go and publish it.

SCENE FIFTEEN

KEVIN'*s office.* BRONWEN *sits waiting for him.* KEVIN *enters.*

BRONWEN: What did he say?
KEVIN: He's going to publish it.
BRONWEN: Terrific.
KEVIN: You'd better come home with me. I don't think they'd
   be stupid enough to try and knock us off, but they could
   try a bit of harassment.
BRONWEN: What makes your place any safer than mine?
KEVIN: Good point.

SCENE SIXTEEN

A seedy motel room. KEVIN *is on the phone.*

KEVIN: What do you mean, too late? It says [*picking up a bro-
   chure*] 'Twenty-four-hour room service' which most
   people take to mean per day, not per month.
   [*Pause.*]
   Look, I'm not asking for a pig's trotters and truffles, just
   oysters. Little snot-like things on shells.
   [*Pause.*]
   Because they stiffen the resolve, dear boy, and I have
   company.
   [*Pause.*]
   Oh yes, very amusing. OK, cut the jokes and just send them
   up. And champagne. French.
BRONWEN: Not French.

KEVIN: Why not?

BRONWEN: Not until they give independence to New Caledonia.

KEVIN: [*into the phone*] Change that to Great Western.
[*Pause.*]
No, I have not just checked my wallet, we have political reasons.
[*He slams the phone down and turns to* BRONWEN. *Pause.*]
That stuff about the oysters was a joke.
[*Pause.*]
On the other hand, I hate to waste a situation.

BRONWEN: No one could ever accuse you of being subtle.

KEVIN: When the mob's out there with their silencers fixed, you tend to feel like a bit of communication. Are you attached to anything?

BRONWEN: No, I'm not. I went through the grisly process of breaking up about a year ago and I haven't been in a hurry to get involved since.

KEVIN: No fun, is it?

BRONWEN: Breaking up? No. I introduced him to a girlfriend of mine just back from New York and I knew it was bad news as soon as they met.

KEVIN: Electricity flowed between them and all that shit.

BRONWEN: My girlfriend had the decency to feel terrible about it.

KEVIN: Not much consolation for you.
[*Pause.*]

BRONWEN: Your boy's back with his mother?

KEVIN: Yeah, she arrived back from the rain forests and took him just when I'd got used to having him around.

BRONWEN: Good kid?

KEVIN: Unbelievable. I know every father says that, but the difference is, I'm right. I just sit and watch him and wonder how a misshapen mental cripple like me could have done it. He's a bloody evolutionary miracle. Have I got a photo? Yes, it just so happens . . .
[*He pulls a small snapshot out of his wallet.*]
The only reason I don't want the hoods out there to shorten my lifespan is so I can have a few more years watching

him grow up.

BRONWEN: [*handing back the photo*] Nice kid.

> [*There is a pause.* KEVIN *takes her hand and kisses it tenderly. She slowly withdraws it like a boot out of a bog.*]

I think I'd better go next door and let you eat your oysters.

KEVIN: I'll get lonely.

BRONWEN: Try the in-house movies.

> [*She exits. He picks up the guide and reads.*]

KEVIN: *Chained Lust! Up and Coming! Daisy Meets the Big Boys!*

> [*He picks up the phone.*]

Yeah, it's me again. Cancel that order. If your movies are that off, I'm buggered if I'm going to risk your oysters.

> [*The phone rings again.*]

Yes . . . Who is this? . . . You bastards.

> [*He hangs up.*]

Bronwen . . . the bastards have threatened my kid.

SCENE SEVENTEEN

The main office area. KEVIN *looks morose and beaten.* BRONWEN *looks at him.*

BRONWEN: We've put too much time and effort into this to let those thugs bully us out of it now. Kevin, I know how much he means to you and if necessary we'll have him here and mount our own twenty-four-hour guard.

KEVIN: Yeah. Get the thing into the system.

BRONWEN: I know how you feel . . .

KEVIN: Get the bloody thing into the system.

> [NICOLE *walks across to them.*]

NICOLE: I've got a list of articles here I'd like to do but I can see this is not a good time.

KEVIN: No it's not.

NICOLE: I know you're not going to believe this, but I'm glad you're getting the Ingles article into print. But I think you're being unfair to Quest.

KEVIN: He should pick his friends more carefully.

NICOLE: You can be so vindictive, Kevin.

KEVIN: Yeah, I'm vindictive. There are a lot of men out there who are living better than I do and I can live with that. Old school tie — connections — charm — plausibility — I'm not too strong in those areas and that's OK but when they aren't satisfied with all of those advantages and cheat their way to an even better deal, then — yeah — I get very vindictive. Fuck them. And I get even more vindictive because most of the time they get away with it. But occasionally, very occasionally, I win and I feel great. So I'm sorry if I'm putting your rape crisis centres at risk, Nicole, but Gary Quest is down the drain.

NICOLE: I hope you'll accept some of the responsibility when a right-wing government replaces him.

KEVIN: I'll be just as tough on them.

NICOLE: Belconnen won't give you the chance.

[REX *enters the office looking stricken.*]

REX: Justice Morgan has dismissed the case against our Minister for Justice.

KEVIN: [*thunderstruck*] You're kidding?

REX: He said he won't commit anyone for trial on the basis of illegal tapes whose authenticity cannot be verified.

KEVIN: That's crazy. They can do voice prints.

REX: Costello can't be compelled to give them. Sorry, Kevin, but that's the end of your article.

KEVIN: OK. Costello's got off but this article is about Ingles and Quest.

REX: They rely on the same tape evidence.

KEVIN: The bloody law! Someone could strangle my mother in a shopping mall at peak hour and be set free two days later because *one* of the five hundred witnesses had his name spelt wrongly on the charge sheet!

[WARREN *enters.*]

REX: I'm sorry, Kevin. It's bloody ridiculous. I'm just as cut up about it as you are.

WARREN: The Ingles article can't go in now, Kevin. The libel
would finish us.

KEVIN: We've written it. You can't stop it now.

WARREN: Are you crazy? I've got worries enough about
Costello suing us without compounding the disaster with
Ingles and Quest. Give me the article.

[WARREN *grabs the article and tears it up.* KEVIN *watches
speechless.*]

[*To* REX] I want to check all this week's copy personally.

KEVIN: You don't have to go to those bloody lengths.

WARREN: I was insane to ever go along with this. If you dig
deep you'll find dirt on just about everyone. It's time you
learned to leave well enough alone, Kevin. If you don't
you're out.

KEVIN: You sack me, Warren, and I'll go straight to the oppo-
sition and find the dirt on you. And there are plenty of
whispers around, I can tell you.

WARREN: [*turning on* REX] You brought this mad dog into this
establishment, Rex, control him — or you're out too.

KEVIN: Control me? I'm totally controlled. The only evidence
that this society would accept is Costello being handed the
money by Ray Rice on peak hour television.

WARREN: The foundation of the law is: innocent until proven
guilty, and there are good reasons for that and I agree with
them. Stop your bellyaching and work harder and when
you do get something I can print, I'll bloody well print it!

SCENE EIGHTEEN

The news is on the television screen.

RICHARD: [*off*] How do you feel about today's decision on Mr
Costello, Mr Quest?

QUEST: Quite frankly, Richard, I'm delighted. Trial by smear
and innuendo has no part in the democratic process. Better to let a thousand Mr Bigs go free than have a single

citizen found guilty on the basis of dubious, illegally made evidence whose authenticity is highly suspect.

RICHARD: Whether the tapes are illegal or not, Mr Quest, they did suggest that Mr Costello had a case to answer.

QUEST: If you condone illegal telephone tapping, Richard, where does it all end? Would you like your phone tapped? Would you like your private and intimate moments laid bare for public scrutiny? This is a democracy Richard, not a police state.

RICHARD: Do you think this decision will make a difference to the editorial policy of the *Review?*

QUEST: I sincerely hope so, Richard. My information is that Warren Belconnen has been worried about the editorial policy of the *Review* for some time now, and I wouldn't be at all surprised to find some changes made in the near future. I am totally committed to the concept of a free press but I am totally opposed to a gutter press. There is a difference.

RICHARD: Thank you, Mr Quest.

QUEST: Thank you.

SCENE NINETEEN

KEVIN *is joined by* LAURIE *in a garden or park.*

KEVIN: 'The cry of the Little Peoples goes up to God in vain, For the world is given over to the cruel Sons of Cain.'

LAURIE: [*laughing*] You didn't expect me to nail Ingles, did you?

KEVIN: They got Nixon in America.

LAURIE: But that's a democracy.

KEVIN: Would've got the bastard if it hadn't been for that loophole.

LAURIE: No chance. The judge was hand picked.

KEVIN: [*sharply*] Who by? Quest?

LAURIE: [*shaking his head*] No one in particular. Corruption in this State runs on automatic pilot, me old mate. The law can put petty crims behind bars, but it's a joke to the big fellas. I could take you on a tour of this city and show you every mansion that's been paid for by the drug trade and not one of the owners will ever be charged.

KEVIN: Drugs have upped the ante?

LAURIE: Your dirty little street-pushing slime can flash a fifty thousand dollar bribe these days. When I first headed up the squad I asked this young addict why he took it. He looked at me as if I was an idiot and said: 'Have you ever had a six-hour orgasm?'

KEVIN: It's just a matter of education, old son. What sane young man would trade eight hours on an assembly line for a six-hour orgasm?

LAURIE: All right, so life's not great. But it's better than turning into a desperate who'd steal his mum's pension cheque for a fix.

KEVIN: Why make them criminals? Why not let them have it if they want it? It can't be worse than turning this State into a paradise for crims and money men.

LAURIE: Fair go, Kevin, you'd have half the country on the stuff.

KEVIN: You're right. Stupid suggestion. Our industrial efficiency would plummet. We would not be a reliable Japanese trading partner. Sorry — stupid suggestion. What's your solution? Increasing the penalties only puts up the price and makes the desperates even more desperate.

LAURIE: Do you know the really ironic thing — and I don't take any pleasure in this, mate — Quest's son is a druggie.
[KEVIN *looks at him, galvanised.*]

SCENE TWENTY

The main office area. BRONWEN, CRYSTAL *and* NICOLE *are at work on their VDUs.* KEVIN *bursts into the office in a high state of excitement.*

KEVIN: Quest's kid's a druggie. The cops picked him up on Saturday night.

CRYSTAL: Did they charge him?

KEVIN: He was only trying to score but there's no doubt he's hooked. Arm like a dartboard. Everybody pays. The chances are the crim that Costello let out supplied the stuff that got the kid hooked. I want you to write this one, Nicole. Everything. Where he lives. How he lives. Where he gets the money to support the habit. What sort of relationship he has with his father. Everything. If he hates his old man, so much the better.

NICOLE: No thanks, Kevin.

KEVIN: What do you mean 'no thanks'? This is the son of the State Premier.

NICOLE: No.

KEVIN: The story is news, it's legitimate and I want it done.

CRYSTAL: What purpose would it serve, Kevin?

KEVIN: For Christ's sake, we're not in this business to serve purposes. This story is accurate, it's newsworthy and I want it printed.

NICOLE: You're doing it purely out of revenge.

KEVIN: That's right — bugger him. He goes into business partnerships with a guy who makes a million bucks importing heroin.

NICOLE: Quest didn't know it was heroin.

KEVIN: Tough. Let him suffer.

CRYSTAL: He's probably suffering enough. How old is the kid?

NICOLE: Sixteen.

CRYSTAL: Jesus, Kevin.

KEVIN: What is this? A bleeding hearts club?

CRYSTAL: You know how you feel about your son.

BRONWEN: If it was exposing something, or leading somewhere, it would be different.

KEVIN: [to BRONWEN] Oh you're in this too?

CRYSTAL: It just wouldn't achieve anything, Kevin.

KEVIN: News is news. If it's true we print it.

NICOLE: We print it if it's in the public interest.

KEVIN: Who's to decide if it is or not?

NICOLE: We are.

KEVIN: And you've decided it's not?

NICOLE: Yes.

> [*Pause.*]

CRYSTAL: It's scandal sheet stuff, Kevin.

KEVIN: What a gutless lot you turned out to be.

BRONWEN: I'm with you on everything else, Kev, but even Quest's entitled to a bit of privacy. You know how you are about your son.

KEVIN: All right, I'll do it myself. Quest has got to realise that in the end everybody pays.

NICOLE: You're your own worst enemy, Kevin, you really are.

KEVIN: Stick around, Nicole. Rex is looking for someone to edit his revamped yuppie *Review*, and my guess is that you'll fit the bill.

SCENE TWENTY-ONE

KEVIN's *office. A single spot shows him typing. He stops and takes a photo of Alan in both hands. He tears out the letter and throws it into the girls' office.*

KEVIN: It's all yours, Nicole — you bloody barracuda. I resign.

> [KEVIN *puts his typewriter and paper in his case and begins to put on his coat.* CRYSTAL *crashes through the door.*]

You can tell the Women's Standing Committe on Being Nice to Everyone at All Cost that I've been a good boy.

CRYSTAL: Where are you going?

KEVIN: I've resigned.

CRYSTAL: Oh, Kevin!

KEVIN: Tell Nicole that the paper's all hers.

CRYSTAL: You can't just give up!

KEVIN: Nicole's right. If we get rid of this government we'll just get a worse one. What's the use?

CRYSTAL: Pity. I came back to tell you what I heard in the pub.

KEVIN: What?

CRYSTAL: Oh, no. You've resigned.

KEVIN: Don't be *cute*!

CRYSTAL: There's some new information come in on Costello
—but we can handle it.

[*She turns to leave.*]

KEVIN: What information —

CRYSTAL: There's a dealer up on a charge who'll spill the beans
if he can do a reduced sentence deal with the police.
Bronwen got a phone number.

KEVIN: Is she still in the pub?

CRYSTAL: Yep.

KEVIN: Go and get her.

[CRYSTAL *waits.*]

Please?

[CRYSTAL *exits.* KEVIN *unpacks his suitcase and sits.*]
I'm not finished yet, me old mate. I'm not finished yet! *I'm
not finished yet!*

THE END

Also available from Currency Press

EMERALD CITY — David Williamson
A fast-moving, wisecracking commentary on contemporary urban morals, and the rivalries and passions on the road to success. Colin, a screen writer, and Kate, a publisher, move to the fame and fortune of the Emerald City, but there are surprises in store for them both. Kate, 'probably Williamson's finest female role to date', writes Katharine Brisbane, 'emerges as an equal — an equally warm, equally conniving, equally vulnerable fighting partner of the protagonist'.

ESSINGTON LEWIS: I AM WORK — John O'Donoghue
Based on the life of Essington Lewis, the industrialist who was the driving force behind the growth of BHP, the play uses music and lyrics by Allan McFadden to enhance the portrait of this very powerful character.

EUROPE and ON TOP OF THE WORLD — Michael Gow
Two fine plays from the author of *Away*. In *Europe* a young Australian travels in pursuit of an actress with whom he has had a brief affair. The sudden encounter of the old world by the new triggers an emotional series of revelations. *On Top of the World* takes a different perspective on history. In a Gold Coast apartment a family ritual assumes awesome proportions as the dying generation and its lost children together discover a resilient new humanity.

CONTEMPORARY AUSTRALIAN DRAMA — Edited by Peter Holloway. Second Edition.
A collection of articles by critics such as Clive James, Katharine Brisbane, Leonard Radic, H. G. Kippax, Brian Kernan, Margaret Williams and many more, offering the best in literary criticism of our living drama. In addition to the best of the first edition, this volume adds major new writing on Ray Mathew, David Williamson, Dorothy Hewett, Patrick White, John Romeril, Alexander Buzo, Stephen Sewell and Louis Nowra amongst others. Added for the first time as a vital reference is a biographical checklist of seventy playwrights now working in the Australian theatre.

Contact Currency Press, P.O. Box 452, Paddington, NSW 2021 for more information.